THE SHAKESPEARE PLAYS

HENRY VIII

THE SHAKESPEARE PLAYS

AS YOU LIKE IT
HENRY VIII
JULIUS CAESAR
MEASURE FOR MEASURE
RICHARD II
ROMEO AND JULIET

THE SHAKESPEARE PLAYS

Literary Consultant: John Wilders

Henry VIII

MAYFLOWER BOOKS
NEW YORK

Library of Congress Cataloging in Publication Data

Shakespeare, William, 1564–1616.
  Henry VIII.

  (His The BBC Shakespeare)
  1.Henry VIII, King of England, 1491–1547 – Drama.
  I. Wilders, John. II. Title. III. Series: Shakespeare, William,
  1564–1616. Selected works. 1978–
  PR2817.A23 1978 822.3'3 78–24131

ISBN 0–8317–4443–X

*PR
2817
.A23
1979
2 av. 1999*

CONTENTS

PREFACE

Cedric Messina

Although the authorship of *Henry VIII* has been hotly contested, some estimates being as low as one third Shakespeare, two thirds A. N. Other, all the actors in this production were firmly convinced that all *their* lines were written by Shakespeare. The strongest reason for believing in at least a collaboration is that, seven years after his death, two of Shakespeare's friends included the play in the First Folio, published in 1623. In the Folio is a head-title *The Workes of William Shakespeare, containing all his Comedies, Histories and Tragedies: Truely set forth, according to their first Originall. Henry VIII* is a play full of court intrigue and ceremony, and is usually presented with great pomp and circumstance, and indeed on its first performance on 29 June 1613, cannons thundered on an entrance of the King towards the end of the play. They thundered so successfully that the Globe Theatre in which it was being performed caught fire and burned to the ground.

This BBC TV production has been shot entirely on location, in three great English family homes, all connected in some way with Henry VIII, Katharine of Aragon, and Anne Bullen and her family: the moated Leeds Castle, sometimes called the loveliest castle in the world; Penshurst Place, the home of Lord de Lisle, VC, and his ancestors since the mid-sixteenth century; and Hever Castle, the one-time home of the Bullen family. They form the background to this play of the fall of three great personages – the Duke of Buckingham, Katharine of Aragon and Cardinal Wolsey. The play has not been without its critics, and commentators and annotators have all had harsh things to say of its lack of cohesion and form, but it has held the stage for three hundred and fifty years, and in this century the number of productions, both in England and the United States, is very impressive. This production was shot on location, with interruptions, between 27 November 1978 and 7 January 1979.

Shakespeare's plays have been performed not only in theatres, but also in country houses, inns and courtyards, and one of the earliest references to performances was made by William Keeting, a Naval Commander who kept a journal of a voyage to the East Indies in 1607. The entry for 5 September, off the coast of Sierra Leone, refers to a performance of *Hamlet*, and that of 30 September to a performance of *Richard II*, both being staged for Portuguese visitors aboard the East India Company's ship *Dragon*. And so the plays started their triumphant progress of performances throughout the civilised world.

BBC Television is not inexperienced in the presentation of Shakespeare's plays, and indeed as early as 1937, on the first regular television service in the world, it presented a full-length version of *Julius Caesar*. Since then, thirty of the plays have been presented, the more popular ones many times over. Some have been produced in encapsulated form like *An Age of Kings*; some done on location, like *Hamlet* at Elsinore with Christopher Plummer as the Prince and Robert Shaw as Claudius, and *Twelfth Night* at Castle Howard in Yorkshire with Janet Suzman leading the cast as Viola. Studio productions have included *The Tragedy of King Lear*, and *The Merchant of Venice* with Maggie Smith as a memorable Portia. Many productions have been taken from the theatre and translated into television terms, like the Royal Shakespeare Company's *The Wars of the Roses* and The National Theatre Zeffirelli production of *Much Ado About Nothing*.

In the discharging of its many duties as a Public Broadcasting Service the BBC has presented during the last ten years at peak viewing time on BBC 1, on every fourth Sunday night, *Play of the Month*, a series of classical productions ranging from all the major plays of Chekhov to a number of Shavian masterpieces. Aeschylus has been produced in the series, and so have many of the plays of William Shakespeare. So not only in the presentation of Shakespeare, but also in the translation to the screen of the great dramatic statements of all ages and countries, has the BBC demonstrated that it is fully equipped to meet the enormous challenge of *The BBC Television Shakespeare*.

The autumn of 1975 gave birth to the idea of recording the complete canon of the thirty-seven plays of the national playwright. (Thirty-six of the plays were published in the First Folio of 1623, exactly half of which had never been published before. The thirty-seventh is *Pericles, Prince of Tyre*, first published in the Quarto of 1609.) The first memo on the subject of televising all the plays emanated from my office on 3 November 1975, and was addressed to Alasdair Milne, then Director of Programmes, and now Managing Director, Television. We were asking for his blessing on the project. His reply was immediate and enthusiastic, as was that of the present Director-General, Ian Trethowan. This warm response to the idea stimulated us in the Plays Department to explore the possibility of making the plan a reality – six plays per year for six years, with one odd man out. It has been called the greatest project the BBC has ever undertaken.

There followed a succession of meetings, conferences, discussions and logistical quotations from engineers, designers, costume designers, make-up artists, financial advisers, educational authorities, university dons and musicians. The Literary Consultant, Dr John Wilders, was appointed, as was David Lloyd-Jones as Music Adviser. Alan Shallcross was made responsible for the preparation of the texts. On the island of Ischia, off the coast of Italy, Sir William Walton composed the opening fanfare for the title music for the series. Visits were made to the United States of America to finalise coproduction deals, decisions were taken about the length of the presentations to average about two and a half hours per play, and more seriously, the order of their transmission. This was a game played by many interested parties, some suggesting they be presented chronologically, which would have meant the series opening with the comparatively unknown *Henry VI Parts 1, 2 and 3*. This idea was hastily abandoned. A judicious mixture of comedy, tragedy and history seemed the best answer to the problem. It was decided that the English histories, from *Richard II* through all the *Henry IVs, V and VIs* to *Richard III* would be presented in chronological order, so that some day in the not too distant future, the eight plays that form this sequence will be able to be seen in their historical order, a unique record of the chronicled history of that time. The plays that form the first sequence will be *Romeo and Juliet, Richard II, As You Like It, Julius Caesar, Measure for Measure* and *Henry VIII*.

The guiding principle behind *The BBC Television Shakespeare* is to make the plays, in permanent form, accessible to audiences throughout the world, and to bring to these many millions the sheer delight and excitement of seeing them in performance – in many cases, for the first time. For students, these productions will offer a wonderful opportunity to study the plays performed by some of the greatest classical actors of our time. But it is a primary intention that the plays are offered as entertainment, to be made as vividly alive as it is possible for the production teams to make

8

them. They are not intended to be museum-like examples of past productions. It is this new commitment, for six plays of Shakespeare per year for six years, that makes the project unique.

In the thirty-seven plays there are a thousand speaking parts, and they demand the most experienced of actors and the most excellent of directors to bring them to life. In the field of directors we are very fortunate, for many of the brilliant practitioners in this series of plays have had wide experience in the classics, both on television and in the theatre. The directors are responsible for the interpretations we shall see, but as the series progresses it will be fascinating to see how many of the actors take these magnificent parts and make them their own.

It was decided to publish the plays, using the Peter Alexander edition, the same text as used in the production of the plays, and one very widely used in the academic world. But these texts with their theatrical divisions into scenes and acts are supplemented with their television equivalents. In other words we are also publishing the television scripts on which the production was based. There are colour and black and white photographs of the production, a general introduction to the play by Dr John Wilders and an article by Henry Fenwick which includes interviews with the actors, directors, designers and costume designers, giving their reactions to the special problems their contributions encountered in the transfer of the plays to the screen. The volumes include a newly-compiled glossary and a complete cast list of the performers, including the names of the technicians, costume designers and scenic designers responsible for the play.

INTRODUCTION TO
HENRY VIII

John Wilders

In 1623, seven years after Shakespeare's death, John Heminge and Henry Condell, two members of the King's Men, the theatrical company for which he had written and with whom he had himself acted, assembled and published the first collected edition of his plays, the so-called First Folio. The thirty-six plays gathered together in their edition, together with *Pericles* which they did not include, are generally agreed to constitute Shakespeare's complete dramatic works. One of the plays published in the First Folio was *Henry VIII*.

Although during the eighteenth century an occasional scholar or editor commented that the style of certain passages seemed untypical of Shakespeare, *Henry VIII* was, for over two hundred years, assumed to be wholly the work of the great dramatist. In 1850, however, a scholar named James Spedding published an essay, 'Who Wrote Shakespeare's *Henry VIII*?', in which he expressed his conviction that the dialogue had been composed in two quite different and distinct styles, the one full of the vividly complex metaphorical writing characteristic of Shakespeare, the other plainer, less imaginative, and, to use Spedding's own words, 'diffuse and languid'. This latter style he identified as typical of Shakespeare's successor as the principal dramatist to the King's Men, John Fletcher, with whom Shakespeare may have collaborated at about the same time in the writing of another play, *The Two Noble Kinsmen*. *Henry VIII*, Spedding concluded, was not composed wholly by Shakespeare but had been written by the two dramatists in collaboration.

Following the publication of Spedding's essay, the authorship of *Henry VIII* has been the subject of a scholarly debate. Those who believe that it is wholly Shakespeare's work have written of it enthusiastically as a well-constructed, profound and subtle expression of his genius; those who have regarded it as a work of collaboration have complained of its loose construction, unevenness of style and shallowness or inconsistency of characterisation. The scholars who think that Fletcher did have a hand in it, though they have not agreed precisely which or how many scenes were written by him, nevertheless believe that the two playwrights worked together very closely and that scenes written entirely by one alternate with scenes written entirely by the other. Their arguments in favour of joint authorship rest exclusively on their own subjective impressions of the style and, since no other evidence has been, or is likely to be, discovered, the problem will almost certainly never be solved. The strongest evidence in favour of Shakespeare's sole authorship is that the two people most likely to know the truth, the dramatist's former intimate colleagues Heminge and Condell, presumably included *Henry VIII* in the First Folio in the belief that it was entirely his. For convenience I shall, throughout the rest of this Introduction, refer to the author of the play as 'Shakespeare'.

The two basic ingredients of a history play, the dramatic and the historical, are potentially in conflict with each other. A play, like any other work of art, should ideally be shapely, well organised and satisfyingly constructed. It should, as Aristotle said of tragedy, have a beginning, a middle and an end. History, on the other hand, is shapeless. Kings and queens, military and political leaders, rise to power, succeed or fail and are defeated or die in a manner which exhibits no consistent, discernible pattern, and, though the life of an individual has a beginning, a middle and an end, the life of a nation neither starts nor finishes. In *Henry VIII* Shakespeare managed to fulfil his function both as a historian, recording the random succession of events of which he had read in the great history book of his time, the *Chronicles* of Holinshed, and as a dramatist, selecting and arranging these events so that they fell into an orderly, satisfying pattern. The play has at the same time the unity and shapeliness of drama and something of the uncompleted loose-endedness of historical reality.

One way in which he achieves this double effect is by creating the impression that, although his play has a beginning, a middle and an end, nevertheless it consists of only one portion of a continuous historical process which has begun long before the start of the first scene and will continue after the last scene is over. He does so by making his characters recall past events and look forward to events which will occur in the future. The play starts in the aftermath of a spectacular diplomatic occasion, the meeting between Henry VIII and Francis I of France in 1520, a ceremonial encounter known as the Field of the Cloth of Gold, with which the hostilities between the two countries were formally brought to an end. The festivities which accompanied this meeting lasted for about two weeks during which the nobility of both countries, extravagantly clothed and jewelled, were lavishly entertained with banquets, dances and military and dramatic spectacles. The ostentatious splendour of the occasion is described by an eye-witness, the Duke of Norfolk, in the conversation with which the play opens:

> To-day the French,
> All clinquant, all in gold, like heathen gods,
> Shone down the English; and to-morrow they
> Made Britain India: every man that stood
> Show'd like a mine.

The audience receives the impression that they have been thrust immediately into the middle of a historical process which is already in motion. The description of the meeting between the two kings (which turns out to be less important for the development of the plot than its prominent position at the opening leads us to expect) introduces a discussion of the man who arranged it, the Lord Chancellor and Archbishop of York, Cardinal Wolsey. A man of humble origins, Wolsey is, we learn, already the most powerful politician and one of the richest men in the country, is presuming to run the affairs of state independently of the King and, by his ruthless arrogance and accumulation of private wealth, has created enemies.

As the opening scene recalls the past, so the final scene predicts the future. The newly-born princess, Elizabeth, is carried on to the stage from her baptism and Cranmer, the Archbishop of Canterbury, foretells that both she and her successor, James I (who was actually on the throne at the time when the play was first acted), will become models of wisdom and goodness to their subjects who, under their government, will prosper and live in peace:

> Peace, plenty, love, truth, terror,
> That were the servants to this chosen infant,
> Shall then be his, and like a vine grow to him;
> Wherever the bright sun of heaven shall shine,
> His honour and the greatness of his name
> Shall be, and make new nations; he shall flourish,
> And like a mountain cedar reach his branches

To all the plains about him; our children's children
Shall see this and bless heaven.

Yet, although Cranmer's prophecy is calmly optimistic, the dramatic tableau with which *Henry VIII* concludes conveys less reassur-
ing implications which would not be lost on Shakespeare's first
audiences. Cranmer, who has replaced Wolsey as the King's
favourite by the end of the play, later fell from power, like his
predecessor, and during the reign of the next monarch was burned
at the stake. Moreover, as Katharine, Henry's first queen, was
divorced and discarded, so Anne, his second wife and the mother
of Elizabeth, was cast off and sent to the execution block. These
facts were common knowledge to the audience at the Globe theatre
who could not fail to recognise that, although the play might
conclude hopefully, history itself continued to be an unpredictable
and unending series of triumphs and defeats.

Shakespeare also conveys the impression of the continuing
movement of history by making first Buckingham, then the
Queen, then Wolsey and finally Cranmer the focus of our attention. The repeated pattern of their falls from or ascents to power
helps to give the play its dramatic shape, but also conveys the
implication that, as each of these major characters has undergone
an ascent and a decline, so, in the future, other statesmen will
enjoy a brief period of supremacy – what Richard II calls 'a breath,
a little scene, to monarchize, be fear'd, and kill with looks' – before
they, in turn, are overtaken by their rivals. Buckingham, the Lord
High Constable and a descendant of Edward III, is executed for
allegedly aspiring to the throne; Queen Katharine, the daughter of
the King of Spain, finds herself a victim of Wolsey's enmity and
Henry's troubled conscience, is discarded and dies in retirement;
Wolsey, his avarice and duplicity exposed by the enemies he has
himself created, is suddenly thrust from power and dies in
obscurity; and although Cranmer is in the ascendant at the close of
the play, the firmly established pattern of power and decline make
us feel little confidence that he will remain permanently in favour.
Wolsey's embittered complaint at the moment of his downfall has
an application to the fates of all these characters:

O, how wretched
Is that poor man that hangs on princes' favours!
There is betwixt that smile we would aspire to,
That sweet aspect of princes, and their ruin
More pangs and fears than wars or women have.

Within the continuing movement of history portrayed in *Henry VIII*, the personal tragedies of Buckingham, Katharine and Wolsey are contained. The audience is invited, in the words of the Prologue, to observe 'How soon this mightiness meets misery'.

Most of Shakespeare's other historical plays are constructed in a similar way. In *Richard II* the decline and death of the King are accompanied by the rise to power of Bolingbroke, and in the two parts of *Henry IV*, while Prince Hal matures steadily towards his accession to the throne, Falstaff grows visibly old and is discarded, and the King sickens and dies. Similarly in *Julius Caesar*, Rome is first dominated by Caesar himself, then, briefly, by his murderers Cassius and Brutus, who in turn are outwitted and defeated by Mark Antony, and as that play concludes we are given the first hints of the ultimate supremacy of Octavius, as yet a subsidiary character in the drama. In all these historical plays Shakespeare enables us to watch events from two conflicting points of view, that of the men of power themselves who devote themselves to the fulfilment of their ambitions and attempt to control history in accordance with their own desires, and that of the all-seeing dramatist who is able to observe their careers in a much broader historical context which makes their aspirations and achievements seem short-lived, precarious and trivial. 'If you consider the infinite extent of eternity', wrote the philosopher Boethius, with whose writings Shakespeare was probably familiar, 'what satisfaction can you have about the power of your name to endure?'

In their moments of defeat or imminent death, Buckingham, Katharine and Wolsey are induced to examine their lives in this wider context, to recognise the pettiness of worldly success and to prepare themselves for the eternal life on which they are about to embark. As the ascents and falls of the major characters provide the play's basic dramatic pattern and shape, so their speeches of self-examination provide its moments of greatest emotional and moral intensity. Although their characters and situations are very different – Katharine is wholly innocent, Buckingham's guilt or innocence are left uncertain, and Wolsey is patently self-indulgent and corrupt – their states of mind in defeat are not dissimilar. In the process of losing their power and possessions they achieve a more secure and satisfying inner calm and stability.

Stripped of his titles, Buckingham nevertheless sees himself as richer than his 'base accusers that never knew what truth meant', and, though condemned to death, as he protests, unjustly, he yet believes that 'Heaven has an end in all'. The Queen, though she asserts her innocence and sees herself as the victim of Wolsey's enmity, also puts her trust in God:

Heaven is above all yet; there sits a Judge
That no king can corrupt.

This disenchantment with the devious ways of the world and consequent trust in the providence of God is expressed even more eloquently by Wolsey who, in defeat, undergoes a swift and radical transformation of character. The man who aspired to become Pope counsels his servant Cromwell to 'fling away ambition' as profitless, recognises that 'corruption wins not more than honesty' and, in the very moment of his crisis, confesses that he has never been 'so truly happy':

I know myself now, and I feel within me
A peace above all earthly dignities,
A still and quiet conscience. The King has cur'd me.

The process whereby Wolsey finds fulfilment in disgrace is later reported by Griffith:

His overthrow heap'd happiness upon him;
For then, and not till then, he felt himself,
And found the blessedness of being little.
And, to add greater honours to his age
Than man could give him, he died fearing God.

In the moments of tragic introspection these characters are forced to undergo, material and political success appear worthless in comparison with personal integrity, faith in God's, rather than their own, will, and the tranquillity of mind which accompanies such virtues.

Shakespeare makes this distinction between worldly power and inner peace of mind not simply by means of the plot but by interspersing scenes of public ceremony with scenes of private, intimate conversation. Katharine makes a powerful public appearance in the council chamber defying Wolsey, but is later portrayed in retirement with her servant Griffith; Anne, having been depicted as a private person, confiding in the old lady, is next seen processing in state to her coronation, and Wolsey, after his appearances as Chancellor and judge, is left in defeat to reveal his private thoughts to Cromwell. In all these secluded, intimate episodes, public affairs are looked at with detachment, at a distance. Anne's attitude to power before her sudden advancement is similar to that of Katharine and Wolsey in decline:

> I swear, 'tis better to be lowly born
> And range with humble livers in content
> Than to be perk'd up in a glist'ring grief
> And wear a golden sorrow.

The various aristocrats and gentlemen who gossip excitedly about the splendour of official ceremonies such as the coronation and the baptism are enraptured by these exterior shows, but the public figures themselves, in their intimate, confessional moments, reveal the anxieties which such displays conceal.

The most striking dramatic feature of *Henry VIII* is, however, its many scenes of elaborate public ceremony, both displayed and reported: the description of the Field of the Cloth of Gold and of Anne's coronation, and the spectacles of Wolsey's banquet, Katharine's trial and Anne's coronation procession. The stage directions for these scenes in the Folio text are unusually detailed, and both these and an account of what must have been one of the earliest performances of the play indicate that it was lavishly produced. In a letter written in July 1613, Sir Henry Wotton reports that a new play has just been acted 'representing some principal pieces of the Reign of *Henry 8*, which was set forth with many extraordinary circumstances of Pomp and Majesty . . . the Knights of the Order, with their Georges and Garter, the Guards with their embroidered Coats and the like'. Yet at their moments of deepest insight, the major characters recognise the unimportance of worldly goods and the precariousness of that temporal power which ceremony symbolises: 'Vain pomp and glory of this world, I hate ye', cries Wolsey in defeat. The displays of pageantry characteristic of *Henry VIII*, though they may entertain the audience, are not included for that purpose alone but are a means of conveying the play's central idea: they are shown in order to be seen through. *Henry VIII* is a play about the glamour of power and its ultimate triviality.

The one character who remains secure through all the political crises and shifts of power is the King. Critics hostile to the play have complained that he is an indistinct, tentatively sketched character and they try to account for Shakespeare's apparent uncertainty about the King by suggesting that the dramatist was compelled for political reasons to conceal the faults of the father of Queen Elizabeth and the inaugurator of English Protestantism. It is true that, in comparison with the fiercely righteous Katharine and the lordly, self-assured Wolsey, Henry makes a less forceful dramatic impression. Moreover, since he undergoes no drastic crisis, his emotions are less fully exposed. Nevertheless his is a disturbing presence. He is impulsive, vigorous, affectionate towards the wife he feels bound in conscience to cast off, loyal and warm-hearted towards his counsellors Wolsey and Cranmer as long as they appear trustworthy, but sudden and decisive in his condemnation of the former once his treachery has been exposed. Shakespeare gives the impression that Henry is a man of action, an extrovert, irritable and testy when the ecclesiastics prolong the divorce proceedings, and embarrassed when circumstances compel him to reveal in public his moral scruples about his marriage to Katharine. Like many apparent extroverts he keeps his intimate feelings hidden, which is why his sudden bursts of irritation or affection are so unpredictable. During the course of the play Henry grows in independence and shrewdness. He makes his first appearance 'leaning on the Cardinal's shoulder' and is totally taken in by Wolsey's flattery and apparent care for the state but, by the end of the play, he sees through the accusations of Cranmer's enemies to the Archbishop's essential goodness and single-handedly undertakes his protection. It is the King's presence which gives continuity to *Henry VIII* and we can also see in this youthful, assertive, quick-tempered monarch the man who degenerated into a tyrant.

It is generally agreed that *Henry VIII* was the last play Shakespeare wrote (or to which he contributed) and that it was completed in 1613, immediately after the four 'romances', *Pericles, Cymbeline, The Winter's Tale* and *The Tempest*. Those critics who believe that Shakespeare wrote all of it have supported their argument by pointing out its resemblances to these other late plays. All of them require elaborate visual and musical effects in production. There is also an emphasis on the virtues of the younger generation (Florizel and Perdita in *The Winter's Tale*, Ferdinand and Miranda in *The Tempest*, the infant Elizabeth in *Henry VIII*) under whose future influence the country will enjoy a stability which the old have failed to achieve, and a belief by the characters that divine providence works steadily for good through the vicissitudes of history. In this final play, even if he was no more than its co-author, Shakespeare was writing on subjects which we know had preoccupied him towards the end of his working life.

THE PRODUCTION

Henry Fenwick

Everyone involved with the television production of *Henry VIII* seems to have been taken by surprise by the play as they worked on it. It is not a play with a good reputation today, as the producer Cedric Messina acknowledges. 'There's a curious, ambivalent attitude towards it, mainly because a lot of people think he didn't write much of it, and that therefore there's something wrong with it. There isn't anything wrong with it and I suspect he wrote more than people think. Seven years after his death I don't think the editors of the Folio would have put in a play in which he had only an infinitesimal amount of work. It's not complimentary to his friends to think they would make such a terrible mistake.' He pauses, then typically adds a rider: 'On the other hand they forgot the thirty-seventh play so I don't know . . .. I would be hard pressed to say what Shakespeare had written and what he hadn't, and I don't think it matters. It is a rather careful look at a period very, very close to the people who were living at the time and for whom he was writing. There are extraordinary things in it – because of course he was walking a tightrope the whole time. There are the sycophantic speeches of Cranmer in praise of the baby Elizabeth at the end, but the portrait of Katharine is a wonderful picture of a discarded woman: she doesn't lose her dignity at all and in her death scene she has one of the most affecting lines in Shakespeare, when she wills to her servants "something over to remember me by". Of course if you've got thirty-seven plays to do some are better than others, but it's my suspicion that in production, with an extremely good cast like this one, they're going to find it's a better play than they thought.'

So far his suspicions are confirmed. The script editor, Alan Shallcross, has certainly been surprised as the play unfolded in rehearsal. 'I'd seen it once,' he recalls, 'with Alexander Knox as Wolsey and Gwen Ffrangcon-Davies as Katharine and my memories were simply of the set pieces. I remembered it as a statuesque piece of ritual, nothing more. The extraordinary thing to find in working on it was that each scene had a dynamic that I had simply not remembered from the theatre. I have a strong feeling that this is one of the plays which will come alive on television in a way they don't in the theatre. I do think the problems of staging the play create a tendency to observe the form rather than the content. The temptation to see only the outward form of the play in the theatre is much greater than in television, where you really have to go in on it.

'All of us, I think, who worked on the play came to it thinking "Oh, this is one of the ones that's never done: we'd better get it over and done with", but it's been immensely rewarding. I approached the text in that spirit and therefore thinking "Well, a lot of this has got to go", but in fact the only cut is the scene which immediately precedes the christening of the baby Princess Elizabeth. It's a scene which I suspect was inserted as a bit of comic relief. It takes place outside the hall in which the christening takes place, between the doorkeeper and the poor people who are thronging the streets to welcome the baby. It is filled with contemporary references and Kevin [Billington, the director] felt, and I agreed with him, that it held up the play at that moment. Its dramatic purpose is to create a link between all the high-born persons whose fortunes we've followed and the ordinary people. The common people of England are not in evidence at all in the play – the gentlemen who form a sort of chorus are aristocrats and the common people are only represented in this one scene. It caused John Wilders [the literary adviser] quite a bit of heart searching and he made a strong plea to retain it, but Kevin felt that telling the story on television was not the same as telling the story in the theatre. You have to have the scene in the theatre if for no other reason than that people have to change clothes. It's a classic example of needing a scene with only about two people in front of the tabs while everybody else is getting ready for the big walk down at the end. In television of course you don't need that.'

The play, Shallcross points out, is 'one of the first attempts to write a play about recent history in a way in which people were represented almost precisely. You have to remember that there would have been in the audience in 1613 at the Globe people whose parents would have been alive during Henry's reign. It's rather like people today, in say their forties and fifties, watching something about Edward VII: their parents would have been alive at that time. The majority of the audience, while they may not have lived through the events, would certainly have known of them through their parents. It was very much part of their recent history. The mere fact that the text does have quite lengthy descriptions of the big ceremonial scenes and that what people wore is actually set down makes it quite obvious Shakespeare's intention was not just to write a play about emotions and relationships and tensions, but actually to represent history for everybody to see. Here in this play for the first time the outward forms are made part of the documentation and I think that is undoubtedly carried through into all the characters and everything they do. There is a bit of tape-recording going on!'

In spite of the 'tape-recording' historical events are switched around and time compressed in the action of the play. 'If you're writing a drama documentary, which this very much is, spanning thirteen to fourteen years, then it is inevitable that there will be an elision of the historical events, and on the whole I don't think it matters one jot. We have a marvellous scene which in the text is the end of a much longer scene which we've split up considerably. The events of that long scene actually took place over a period of years and in the theatre it tends to tail off into a two-hander between Wolsey and Cromwell, his faithful servant. We have taken it away, relocated it – we recorded it in the crypt at Penshurst – and made it very much separate in feel and place and rhythm. That also helps underline the fact that the meeting between Cromwell and Wolsey actually took place very much later, in a convent outside London at a time when Wolsey was withdrawn from the court. It actually makes much more sense of the text: here is a man who has been right in the centre of the court suddenly absent from it, who still has this extraordinary interest in what's going on. Rather like a man who's retired from business and six months later some man comes down from head office to see him and he still wants to know who's in charge, whether so and so is still running the pension fund . . . that sort of thing. We've been able to do what you can never do on stage, to put back some of the passage of chronological time simply because we have the magic carpet of television. By relocating and refocusing the scene it becomes immensely strong – Cromwell warned by Wolsey, who is drawing on his own experience. Of course the irony is that a Jacobean audience would have known how Cromwell did in fact rise later. Undoubtedly Shakespeare's documentary approach is nudging the audience into seeing contemporary relevance in all that he chooses to show.'

The language of *Henry VIII*, too, poses fewer problems for

television than does that of the early Shakespeare plays, which are richer in rhetoric and descriptive verse. 'The Globe Theatre wasn't representational, while what television is doing is being literal, and there is a conflict between that and the poetry. In *Henry VIII* there's practically no poetry at all – it's documentary land. The language is spare and tough, very much late Shakespeare, full of greys and browns. It's lean, there's no sunshine at all. It is also very much the language of politicians, of people jockeying for power, striking attitudes, using words not only for their meaning but also for their effect.'

Director Kevin Billington had never seen the play and found very few people, he says, who did know it. 'I found that the immediate reaction was "Oh, yes, that's the one with all the pageants and the two great speeches." I thought, "Gosh, I'm not going to do 'Henry's Twenty Golden Moments'", but that is how people think of it – not as a play but as fine moments. That's what worried me. When you first read it it does look like a great pageant, but the more you work on it the more you find that the pageant side is there for you to see through.' The more he worked on it, too, the more uncuttable he found it: 'It's extremely easy to cut if what you want to do is make it move on, but if you actually want to do Shakespeare's play it's very, very difficult – two or three lines cut make something else work not so well.

'I recently met Peter Hall [Director of the National Theatre], who said, "I hear you're doing *Henry VIII*; I managed to avoid that for twenty years at the RSC." It *is* generally regarded as being second-rate but I think that's a hangover from the Victorian days. The whole attitude is affected because they think it isn't by Shakespeare. And there is very little written about it – apart from one or two good things all the commentary is about who wrote it. I've now come to the conclusion that it's marvellous in 1978/79 to be able to do a Shakespeare play that's not known and that there aren't a million versions of. In the last twenty-five years it's been done twice in London: [Tyrone] Guthrie did it in 1949 and then in 1953, but since then it's been done once at the RSC and once at the Old Vic. That is incredible. Usually there are set conventions and attitudes to the plays and directors either go along very conventionally or feel they have to be extraordinary, whereas I feel with this as though someone put it through the post last night.'

The question of authorship is one Billington resolved to ignore, though the more he worked on the play the more he became convinced that the structure and thought behind it had to be the

work of one man. 'All the people who I thought had the right idea
about the play put it down to Shakespeare. The funny thing was
that the actors – this happened with Tim West and Claire [Bloom]
and John [Stride] and Jeremy Kemp – each one took me on one
side and said, "I know that all this play isn't by Shakespeare but
there's no doubt that my lines are by Shakespeare".'

Billington's first production concern was that the play should be
shot on location: 'I don't think the play would work in a studio – or
let's say I don't think I could make it work in a studio. I wanted to
get away from the idea that this is some kind of fancy pageant. I
wanted to feel the reality: I wanted great stone walls, I wanted
people to lurk in corners, to come out of darkness at the end of
corridors, to go outside to discuss things. I loved doing it in the
winter – not for practical reasons, it's been a nightmare. The
organisation had to be extraordinary because we had to work on
the basis that the light would go at about three – the lighting man
has done a stupendous job. We filmed part of one scene one day
then it snowed during the night! But for atmosphere it was
marvellous. When Buckingham went to his death he had to go off
in a boat and we had to break the ice to give the boat a channel to
go through. But once we'd broken the ice and the boat was sailing
through it – and we filmed it at about three in the afternoon when
the light was going, so they had to play with their technical gear –
and the actor's face was all drawn in the cold . . . it was
marvellous.

'We shot at Hever Castle, where Anne Bullen lived; at Penshurst, which was Buckingham's place; and at Leeds Castle, where
Henry was with Anne Bullen. The actors were never out of rooms
that were 400 or 500 years old. You couldn't possibly build the sets
we've got. That doesn't mean I've got a lot of walking about to
show off the locations – the thing has to go at a terrific crack. I
suppose because I've worked on location in films a lot I don't feel
I've got to "use" locations in that silly way by having a lot of
opening doors and walking down corridors. I try to catch the
reality that locations can give.'

Using such authentic locations made the designers' jobs at once
easier and more difficult. Don Taylor, who also worked on the sets
of *As You Like It*, believes in being self-effacing. Indeed, not only
does he feel that he should simply provide fitting settings for the
actors and not project his own vision obtrusively on to them, he
also clearly dislikes being talked to about his work. The main task
for him, with such authentic interiors, was to make sure that any

additions – such as the King's dais he had erected in the great hall of Penshurst, where the arraignment is being enacted – blend unobtrusively with the reality, colours and textures being of paramount importance. He and Magda Olender, in charge of finding the right props, have done a job of massive discretion.

Alun Hughes, the costume designer, is pleased, too, with the way his costumes blend in on location: 'The clothes come to life in these castles. It's a good period, the Tudor period, because there's a lot of evidence about what they wore, a lot of lovely paintings, definite patterns, definite colours. One has a pretty good idea of the look of it all. But when it comes to details there's quite a lot of research needed to get it right. With the jewellery I found it was quite a good cheat to have pinned brooches made – about 160 of different types. Then I'd use the same tunic but change the jewellery – I'd take one lot off, change the sleeves and put another lot on for a different scene and it made at least two garments out of one. In fact they were very thrifty in that period – which is useful on our budget! The clothes were structured, very hardy and lasted an awfully long time, so that you could add bits and pieces and the basic thing stayed. It was the men who made the clothes in those days, the women did all the fine embroidery, the bits and pieces that went with them. For Katharine of Aragon's frocks or Anne Bullen's you'd have a basic simple dress, then you'd change the sleeves and the underdress. If you notice, down the seams of the bodices there are little brass or silver pins – in fact they were nailed. If they got torn it became fashionable to use another material, so you'd get the slashed sleeve with the shirt pulled out: very much a recycling. They would have jewels given to them and sew them into a frock, then later they'd take them off and put them on another. That was their wealth and they wore it all the time.' He has used some of the same recycling tricks himself, mixing clothes that have been hired with stuff salvaged from BBC stock. 'There's a bit of everything, begged, borrowed and stolen! A lot of Nathan's older stock has lasted well and I've hired that from them, and sometimes I've added fur or cuffs off old clothes that we had in stock already.'

He hovers around the shooting for last-minute touch-ups that he feels are crucial: 'I'm painting stuff as the actors are going on. Sometimes the braid and the jewels sparkle a bit too much, look too new. In one scene the other day we did a very long shot of the king and queen on their thrones. Claire just moved her head very slightly and there was a great sparkle in her head-dress that was very nice for that scene, but this morning I noticed that as she walked up to Henry's throne her cross was dazzling, distracting in the solemnity of the trial scene, so I got my brush and painted it down a bit. These sort of little bits and pieces all contribute.

'You sometimes have to use your imagination in the designing – for instance, when Henry meets Anne Bullen he's described as being in masquerade, dressed as a shepherd in cloth of gold. Well, a shepherd in cloth of gold would be a funny sight. I just did a very simple chamarre, a cape that's just a fold of material with a slit for the head, that pattern in gold cloth. I thought that maybe they just thought, "We'll do this for a lark, get a bit of that curtain that's hanging there, cut it up and dress up for a lark" – and that's the way I treated it.'

Most of the actors did a great deal of historical research into their characters, in spite of the fact that historical knowledge often has to be discarded. 'As always with Shakespeare, you have to throw a lot of it out of the window because the historical character is not Shakespeare's character,' says Timothy West. 'But I prefer to do the research first so that it's all there, then you know what's going to be useful and what you're going to have to jettison. I've found the most interesting book I read was by George Cavendish, who was Wolsey's gentleman usher. He wrote at a safe distance after Wolsey's death: he got all his notes together – out of presumably a *very* good hiding place – and once or twice he says, "My old muddled wits let me down at this stage . . . I don't really remember the details of this", and you know something pretty horrendous went on. He obviously loved and respected Wolsey terrifically and gives a wonderful insight into Wolsey's behaviour. He's quite critical of him but to have a blow-by-blow account by the man on the spot is terrific: it's the kind of biography you don't normally get, delving that far back into history.'

The great difficulty for us today in understanding Wolsey, he feels, is the lack of any contemporary terms of reference for a figure of Wolsey's power: 'somebody who was not only head of the church – he wasn't Archbishop of Canterbury, he was Archbishop of York, but he made himself top man over the Archbishop of Canterbury by having a special deal with the Pope – but also Lord Chancellor and the equivalent of Prime Minister and head of ICI and head of an international banking company. When you read an account of the number of people he employed and took with him when he stayed anywhere, it's fantastic. And we today, I think, have difficulty reconciling this with the attitudes of a churchman.

But in those days the church was very powerful and had to be seen to be powerful or it didn't work.'

When he came to this production, although he had never played the part of Wolsey on stage, Timothy West had recorded a few speeches from it and done some in recitals. 'I'd seen the play but you very seldom get the chance to do it. I think we have discovered a lot about it. We most of us think it's a good play for television because it isn't a play of enormous rhetoric. It's a play where thoughts change very rapidly and there's an awful lot the television camera can help you with, which perhaps would need a lot of work to get over on stage.

'It's not just a mini-play about intrigue – it deals with things on a very high metaphysical level and it has an overall grand design that I think it's important to pay respect to. Nearly all Shakespeare's histories, as well as most of his tragedies, treat with the person after whom the play is named right up to their death. *Richard II* does, *Henry IV* does, *Richard III* does, *Henry VI* does; but *Henry V* doesn't and *Henry VIII* doesn't and I think there are interesting parallels. Both stop at a kind of moment of triumph in the subject's life. If you think of *Henry V* as tracing the development of a man and the finding of himself through experience and through suffering and a sense of duty, to a lesser extent *Henry VIII* does the same thing. It leaves Henry when he's got all the threads together. You start by thinking this man isn't going to manage but it leaves the play at the birth of a golden age, everything is at its zenith and you feel yes, this man is going to be able to cope. The various threatening things have been settled and the people like Wolsey, who have been a threat, have departed not in an ignoble, ignominious way but with a terrific dignity and grandeur.

'For some people the play does divide into sections a little crudely, but for every falling cadence you get a rising one coming up under it, almost like a musical score. As Wolsey falls, Cranmer rises; as Katharine falls, Anne rises; as Buckingham falls there is a resurgence of baronial feeling. It's like a set of variations created by a very brilliant variationist.'

Claire Bloom remembers seeing Gwen Ffrangcon-Davies as Katharine in the production that celebrated the Queen's coronation in 1953, 'and I'm equally sure I can hear Dame Edith's voice doing it – I think I must have seen her, unless I only heard it on the radio. I'd always been fascinated by Katharine of Aragon and I think the most helpful book was Garrett Mattingly's, which I had read a long time before. But there's only so much research you can incorporate. You can't play an historical character unless you know the background, but once you've got past a certain point then research is as much for pleasure as anything else. I think the most interesting thing, which I simply didn't know at all, was that their marriage had been such a remarkable one for so long. One rather thinks she was married to him because his older brother died and that eventually he tired of her and cast her off, but one did not know of the years between, of the jousts when he wore her colours, of the poetry he wrote to her, his absolute adoration of her, or that she had been pretty as a young girl. I'm afraid one does think of her as an old bag in a gable head-dress but she was rather charming and loved to dance. Life took it out of her – as it does.'

But the quality that attracted and impressed Miss Bloom most of all was, she says, Katharine's pride: 'Her tremendous pride and dignity in the worst circumstances that can happen to a woman, which has not changed between then and now – a woman reaching middle age being put aside for a younger woman. Obviously there were very many other reasons for it, but basically he fell in love with a young woman and Katharine was six years older and he didn't want her any more. Yet she never lost her love for him. She always adored him and never said a word against him till the very end – ever. What makes her different from any other wife who happens to be put aside is that she was the daughter of their most Catholic Majesties Ferdinand and Isabella of Spain, so that in no way could she compromise in her mind or in her deed with the question of a divorce or separation or annulment. Her position is quite impossible. And apart from all those high-falutin reasons it's a smashing part, and though she only has four scenes they come in the right place and each one's wonderful.'

John Stride had seen both the 1953 production and 'once before when I was a very young boy', and the impressions he had carried away with him were of 'a golden Henry and a purple Wolsey' but otherwise his memories were hazy. He was on a cruise off the Canaries when he was offered the part but luckily the ship's library had a complete Shakespeare so he was able to refresh his memory immediately. It's not, however, a play that springs off the page and it was only in working on it that he was able to get the measure of the role. A central problem was resolving Henry's feelings and attitudes about Katharine. Shakespeare treads warily, leaving much for the actor to flesh out. 'There had been twenty-five years of marriage and very happy ones too. But he needed a son and he had to balance his responsibilities to the kingdom with his personal affection. There's one part I'm still not sure about. He's talking about Kate and he says:

> Would it not grieve an able man to leave
> So sweet a bedfellow? But, conscience, conscience!
> O, 'tis a tender place! and I must leave her.

I'm not sure whether he really loves her then or whether he is making an excuse for his actions. *I* genuinely meant it. Nowhere does Shakespeare say Henry was wrong or that he was a schemer.

'There's a clear line of development in the play – in the opening scene Henry is leaning on Wolsey's shoulder and I think that's symbolic. At the end he's standing on his own, carrying the baby Elizabeth. It's a picture of growing strength. Obviously he was a very strong man who hadn't really flexed his muscles, but by the end of the play he has taken over.'

'He goes from being a king who reigns to a king who rules,' says Kevin Billington. 'He's young at the beginning, impulsive, quick-tempered, he doesn't think things through; but as the play goes on his decisions tend to get righter and righter. I think he's a man who actively cared about Kate but it's the throne that mattered.' In his direction Billington has tried to make clearer the play's focus on Henry's development: 'During the prologue I'm setting the scene in the great council chamber and as the prologue continues we're tracking down the hall and you realise someone is sitting on the throne at the end. The shot finishes on a close-up, not of the young Henry but the old. It's as though the whole play is a flashback.

'It's also a play about dying, about how you face your maker. As it says in the prologue it's about mightiness meeting misery. It's Shakespeare's last play and there's a fascination with men in power fighting and struggling but then facing God. They all have good deaths – Buckingham, Wolsey, Katharine. For a protestant play-wright in the early seventeenth century to write about a Catholic Spaniard as if she was a saint is astonishing. And absolutely fundamental to an understanding of the play is the belief that there is some reconciliation, you can actually face your maker. And through the suffering, through the deaths, through the complications the nation comes through to our new religion and our new queen. I don't think people look at the play in the right way – you have to accept certain Christian basics. It's a play that deserves looking at again. I'm hoping that this production will set people off trying to see how they can do it in the theatre. That would be a wonderful thing for television to do.'

THE BBC TV CAST AND PRODUCTION TEAM

The cast for the BBC television production was as follows:

KING HENRY	John Stride
CARDINAL WOLSEY	Timothy West
QUEEN KATHARINE	Claire Bloom
CRANMER, ARCHBISHOP OF CANTERBURY	Ronald Pickup
GARDINER, BISHOP OF WINCHESTER	Peter Vaughan
DUKE OF BUCKINGHAM	Julian Glover
DUKE OF NORFOLK	Jeremy Kemp
ANNE BULLEN	Barbara Kellermann
CROMWELL	John Rowe
CARDINAL CAMPEIUS	Michael Poole
BISHOP OF LINCOLN	David Dodimead
LORD SANDYS	Charles Lloyd Pack
LORD CHAMBERLAIN	John Nettleton
DUKE OF SUFFOLK	Lewis Fiander
EARL OF SURREY	Oliver Cotton
LORD ABERGAVENNY	David Rintoul
LORD CHANCELLOR	Jack May
SIR HENRY GUILDFORD	Adam Bareham
SIR THOMAS LOVELL	Nigel Lambert
SIR NICHOLAS VAUX	Jack McKenzie
DR BUTTS	John Rogan
GRIFFITH	John Bailey
PATIENCE	Sally Home
OLD LADY	Sylvia Coleridge
A GIRL	Emma Kirkby
CAPUCHIUS	John Rhys-Davies
1ST GENTLEMAN	John Cater
2ND GENTLEMAN	Roger Lloyd Pack
A SURVEYOR	David Troughton

SERGEANT AT ARMS	Alan Leith
DOOR-KEEPER	Brian Osborne
PAGE TO GARDINER	Timothy Barker
A CRIER	Michael Gaunt
A MESSENGER	Michael Walker
A SERVANT	Jeffrey Daunton
A SCRIBE	Jeffrey Daunton
THE SPEAKER	Tony Church
CHOREOGRAPHER	Geraldine Stephenson
PRODUCTION ASSISTANTS	Joan Hamilton
	Terence Banks
PRODUCTION UNIT MANAGERS	Fraser Lowden
	Alan Hiley
MUSIC	James Tyler
MUSIC ADVISER	David Lloyd-Jones
LITERARY CONSULTANT	John Wilders
MAKE-UP ARTIST	Dawn Alcock
COSTUME DESIGNER	Alun Hughes
SOUND	Ian Lieper
LIGHTING	Hugh Cartwright
DESIGNER	Don Taylor
SCRIPT EDITOR	Alan Shallcross
PRODUCER	Cedric Messina
DIRECTOR	Kevin Billington

Produced on location at Leeds Castle, near Maidstone, Kent, Penshurst Place, Penshurst, Kent, and Hever Castle, Edenbridge, Kent, between 27 November 1978 and 7 January 1979.

THE TEXT

In order to help readers who might wish to use this text to follow the play on the screen the scene divisions and locations used in the television production and any cuts and rearrangements made are shown in the right-hand margins. The principles governing these annotations are as follows:

1. Where a new location (change of set) is used by the TV production this is shown as a new scene. The scenes are numbered consecutively, and each one is identified as exterior or interior, located by a brief description of the set of the location, and placed in its 'time' setting (e.g. Day, Night, Dawn). These procedures are those used in BBC Television camera scripts.

2. Where the original stage direction shows the entry of a character at the beginning of a scene, this has not been deleted (unless it causes confusion). This is in order to demonstrate which characters are in the scene, since in most cases the TV scene begins with the characters 'discovered' on the set.

3. Where the start of a TV scene does not coincide with the start of a scene in the printed text, the characters in that scene have been listed, *unless* the start of the scene coincides with a stage direction which indicates the entrance of all those characters.

4. Where the text has been cut in the TV production, the cuts are marked by vertical rules and by a note in the margin. If complete lines are cut these are shown as, e.g., Lines 27–38 omitted. If part of a line only is cut, or in cases of doubt (e.g. in prose passages), the first and last words of the cut are also given.

5. Occasionally, and only when it is thought necessary for comprehension of the action, a note of a character's moves has been inserted in the margin.

6. Where the action moves from one part of a set to another, no attempt has been made to show this as a succession of scenes.

ALAN SHALLCROSS

HENRY VIII

DRAMATIS PERSONÆ

KING HENRY THE EIGHTH.
CARDINAL WOLSEY.
CARDINAL CAMPEIUS.
CAPUCIUS, *Ambassador from the Emperor Charles V.*
CRANMER, ARCHBISHOP OF CANTERBURY.
DUKE OF NORFOLK.
DUKE OF BUCKINGHAM.
* DUKE OF SUFFOLK.
EARL OF SURREY.
LORD CHAMBERLAIN.
LORD CHANCELLOR.
GARDINER, BISHOP OF WINCHESTER.
BISHOP OF LINCOLN.
LORD ABERGAVENNY.
* LORD SANDYS.
* SIR HENRY GUILDFORD.
SIR THOMAS LOVELL.
* SIR ANTHONY DENNY.
SIR NICHOLAS VAUX.
SECRETARIES *to Wolsey.*
CROMWELL, *servant to Wolsey.*

GRIFFITH, *gentleman-usher to Queen Katharine.*
* THREE GENTLEMEN.
DR. BUTTS, *physician to the King.*
GARTER KING-AT-ARMS.
SURVEYOR *to the Duke of Buckingham.*
* BRANDON, *and a Sergeant-at-Arms.*
DOORKEEPER *of the Council Chamber.*
| PORTER, *and his* MAN.
PAGE *to* GARDINER.
A CRIER.

QUEEN KATHARINE, *wife to King Henry, afterwards divorced,*
ANNE BULLEN, *her Maid of Honour, afterwards Queen.*
AN OLD LADY, *friend to Anne Bullen.*
PATIENCE, *woman to Queen Katharine.*
LORD MAYOR, Aldermen, Lords *and* Ladies *in the Dumb Shows;* Women *attending upon the Queen ;* Scribes, Officers, Guards, *and other* Attendants ; Spirits.

In the television production the parts of the Third Gentleman and Lord Sandys are combined as Lord Sandys.

The parts of the Duke of Suffolk and Brandon are combined as the Duke of Suffolk.

| These parts omitted.

The parts of Sir Henry Guildford and Sir Anthony Denny are combined as Sir Henry Guildford.

THE SCENE : *London ; Westminster ; Kimbolton.*

THE PROLOGUE

I come no more to make you laugh ; things now
That bear a weighty and a serious brow,
Sad, high, and working, full of state and woe,
Such noble scenes as draw the eye to flow,
We now present.   Those that can pity here   5
May, if they think it well, let fall a tear :
The subject will deserve it.   Such as give
Their money out of hope they may believe
May here find truth too.   Those that come to see
Only a show or two, and so agree   10
The play may pass, if they be still and willing,

SCENE I
Interior. London. A Chamber in the Royal Palace. Day.
Voice over shot of King Henry seated alone.

I'll undertake may see away their shilling
Richly in two short hours. Only they
That come to hear a merry bawdy play,
A noise of targets, or to see a fellow   15
In a long motley coat guarded with yellow,
Will be deceiv'd ; for, gentle hearers, know,
To rank our chosen truth with such a show
As fool and fight is, beside forfeiting
Our own brains, and the opinion that we bring   20
To make that only true we now intend,
Will leave us never an understanding friend.
Therefore, for goodness sake, and as you are known
The first and happiest hearers of the town,
Be sad, as we would make ye. Think ye see   25
The very persons of our noble story
As they were living ; think you see them great,
And follow'd with the general throng and sweat
Of thousand friends ; then, in a moment, see
How soon this mightiness meets misery.   30
And if you can be merry then, I'll say
A man may weep upon his wedding-day.

ACT ONE

SCENE I. *London.   The palace.*

Enter the DUKE OF NORFOLK *at one door ; at the other, the*
DUKE OF BUCKINGHAM *and the* LORD ABERGAVENNY.

BUCK. Good morrow, and well met.   How have ye done
Since last we saw in France ?
NOR.   I thank your Grace,
Healthful ; and ever since a fresh admirer
Of what I saw there.
BUCK.   An untimely ague
Stay'd me a prisoner in my chamber when   5
Those suns of glory, those two lights of men,
Met in the vale of Andren.
NOR.   'Twixt Guynes and Arde—
I was then present, saw them salute on horseback ;
Beheld them, when they lighted, how they clung
In their embracement, as they grew together ;   10
Which had they, what four thron'd ones could have weigh'd
Such a compounded one ?
BUCK.   All the whole time
I was my chamber's prisoner.
NOR.   Then you lost
The view of earthly glory ; men might say,
Till this time pomp was single, but now married   15
To one above itself.   Each following day
Became the next day's master, till the last
Made former wonders its.   To-day the French,
All clinquant, all in gold, like heathen gods,
Shone down the English ; and to-morrow they   20
Made Britain India : every man that stood

SCENE 2
Exterior. France. Day.
King Henry and King
Francis meeting ('The
Field of the Cloth of
Gold').

SCENE 3
Exterior. London.
Outside the Royal
Palace. Day.
BUCKINGHAM meets
NORFOLK and
ABERGAVENNY.

Show'd like a mine.   Their dwarfish pages were
As cherubins, all gilt ; the madams too,
Not us'd to toil, did almost sweat to bear
The pride upon them, that their very labour   25
Was to them as a painting.   Now this masque
Was cried incomparable ; and th' ensuing night
Made it a fool and beggar.   The two kings,
Equal in lustre, were now best, now worst,
As presence did present them : him in eye   30
Still him in praise ; and being present both,
'Twas said they saw but one, and no discerner
Durst wag his tongue in censure.   When these suns—
For so they phrase 'em—by their heralds challeng'd
The noble spirits to arms, they did perform   35
Beyond thought's compass, that former fabulous story,
Being now seen possible enough, got credit,
That Bevis was believ'd.

BUCK.   O, you go far !
NOR. As I belong to worship, and affect
      In honour honesty, the tract of ev'rything   40
      Would by a good discourser lose some life
      Which action's self was tongue to.   All was royal :
      To the disposing of it nought rebell'd ;
      Order gave each thing view.   The office did
      Distinctly his full function.

BUCK.   Who did guide—   45
      I mean, who set the body and the limbs
      Of this great sport together, as you guess ?
NOR. One, certes, that promises no element
      In such a business.

BUCK.   I pray you, who, my lord ?
NOR. All this was ord'red by the good discretion   50
      Of the right reverend Cardinal of York.
BUCK. The devil speed him ! No man's pie is freed
      From his ambitious finger.   What had he
      To do in these fierce vanities ?   I wonder
      That such a keech can with his very bulk   55
      Take up the rays o' th' beneficial sun,
      And keep it from the earth.

NOR.   Surely, sir,
      There's in him stuff that puts him to these ends ;
      For, being not propp'd by ancestry, whose grace
      Chalks successors their way, nor call'd upon   60
      For high feats done to th' crown, neither allied
      To eminent assistants, but spider-like,
      Out of his self-drawing web, 'a gives us note
      The force of his own merit makes his way—
      A gift that heaven gives for him, which buys   65
      A place next to the King.

ABER.   I cannot tell
      What heaven hath given him—let some graver eye
      Pierce into that ; but I can see his pride
      Peep through each part of him.   Whence has he that ?
      If not from hell, the devil is a niggard   70

Lines 23–28, 'the
madams too . . . and
beggar', omitted.

Lines 36–38, 'that
former . . . was
believ'd', omitted.

Or has given all before, and he begins
A new hell in himself.
BUCK.   Why the devil,
Upon this French going out, took he upon him—
Without the privity o' th' King—t' appoint
Who should attend on him ?   He makes up the file   75
Of all the gentry ; for the most part such
To whom as great a charge as little honour
He meant to lay upon ; and his own letter,
The honourable board of council out,
Must fetch him in he papers.
ABER.   I do know   80
Kinsmen of mine, three at the least, that have
By this so sicken'd their estates that never
They shall abound as formerly.
BUCK.   O, many
Have broke their backs with laying manors on 'em
For this great journey.   What did this vanity   85
But minister communication of
A most poor issue ?
NOR.   Grievingly I think
The peace between the French and us not values
The cost that did conclude it.
BUCK.   Every man,
After the hideous storm that follow'd, was   90
A thing inspir'd, and, not consulting, broke
Into a general prophecy—that this tempest,
Dashing the garment of this peace, aboded
The sudden breach on't.
NOR.   Which is budded out ;
For France hath flaw'd the league, and hath attach'd   95
Our merchants' goods at Bordeaux.
ABER.   Is it therefore
Th' ambassador is silenc'd ?
NOR.   Marry, is't.
ABER. A proper title of a peace, and purchas'd
At a superfluous rate !
BUCK.   Why, all this business
Our reverend Cardinal carried.
NOR.   Like it your Grace,   100
The state takes notice of the private difference
Betwixt you and the Cardinal.   I advise you—
And take it from a heart that wishes towards you
Honour and plenteous safety—that you read
The Cardinal's malice and his potency   105
Together ; to consider further, that
What his high hatred would effect wants not
A minister in his power.   You know his nature,
That he's revengeful ; and I know his sword
Hath a sharp edge—it's long and't may be said   110
It reaches far, and where 'twill not extend,
Thither he darts it.   Bosom up my counsel,
You'll find it wholesome.   Lo, where comes that rock
That I advise your shunning.

Lines 78–80, 'and his own . . . papers', omitted.

Lines 85–87, 'What did . . . issue', omitted.

Enter CARDINAL WOLSEY, *the purse borne before him, certain of the*
   Guard, *and two* Secretaries *with papers.   The Cardinal in his*
   passage fixeth his eye on BUCKINGHAM, *and* BUCKINGHAM *on him, both*
   full of disdain.
WOL. The Duke of Buckingham's surveyor ? Ha !   115
   Where's his examination ?
I SECR.   Here, so please you. | I SECRETARY is played
WOL. Is he in person ready ?   by CROMWELL.
I SECR.   Ay, please your Grace. |
WOL. Well, we shall then know more, and Buckingham
   Shall lessen this big look.
                                    [*Exeunt* WOLSEY *and his* Train.
BUCK. This butcher's cur is venom-mouth'd, and I   120
   Have not the power to muzzle him ; therefore best
   Not wake him in his slumber.   A beggar's book
   Outworths a noble's blood.
NOR.   What, are you chaf'd ?
   Ask God for temp'rance ; that's th' appliance only
   Which your disease requires.
BUCK.   I read in's looks   125
   Matter against me, and his eye revil'd
   Me as his abject object.   At this instant
   He bores me with some trick.   He's gone to th' King ;
   I'll follow, and outstare him.
NOR.   Stay, my lord,
   And let your reason with your choler question   130
   What 'tis you go about.   To climb steep hills
   Requires slow pace at first.   Anger is like
   A full hot horse, who being allow'd his way,
   Self-mettle tires him.   Not a man in England.
   Can advise me like you ; be to yourself   135
   As you would to your friend.
BUCK.   I'll to the King,
   And from a mouth of honour quite cry down
   This Ipswich fellow's insolence ; or proclaim
   There's difference in no persons.
NOR.   Be advis'd :
   Heat not a furnace for your foe so hot   140
   That it do singe yourself.   We may outrun
   By violent swiftness that which we run at,
   And lose by over-running.   Know you not | Lines 143–145, 'Know
   The fire that mounts the liquor till't run o'er | you . . . wastes it',
   In seeming to augment it wastes it ?   Be advis'd.   145 | omitted.
   I say again there is no English soul
   More stronger to direct you than yourself,
   If with the sap of reason you would quench
   Or but allay the fire of passion.
BUCK.   Sir,
   I am thankful to you, and I'll go along   150
   By your prescription ; but this top-proud fellow—
   Whom from the flow of gall I name not, but
   From sincere motions, by intelligence,
   And proofs as clear as founts in July when
   We see each grain of gravel—I do know   155

To be corrupt and treasonous.
NOR.   Say not treasonous.
BUCK. To th' King I'll say't, and make my vouch as strong
    As shore of rock.   Attend : this holy fox,
    Or wolf, or both—for he is equal rav'nous
    As he is subtle, and as prone to mischief   160
    As able to perform't, his mind and place
    Infecting one another, yea, reciprocally—
    Only to show his pomp as well in France
    As here at home, suggests the King our master
    To this last costly treaty, th' interview   165
    That swallowed so much treasure and like a glass
    Did break i' th' wrenching.
NOR.   Faith, and so it did.
BUCK. Pray, give me favour, sir ; this cunning cardinal
    The articles o' th' combination drew
    As himself pleas'd ; and they were ratified   170
    As he cried ' Thus let be ' to as much end
    As give a crutch to th' dead.   But our Count-Cardinal
    Has done this, and 'tis well ; for worthy Wolsey,
    Who cannot err, he did it.   Now this follows,
    Which, as I take it, is a kind of puppy   175
    To th' old dam treason : Charles the Emperor,
    Under pretence to see the Queen his aunt—
    For 'twas indeed his colour, but he came
    To whisper Wolsey—here makes visitation—
    His fears were that the interview betwixt   180
    England and France might through their amity
    Breed him some prejudice ; for from this league
    Peep'd harms that menac'd him—privily
    Deals with our Cardinal ; and, as I trow—
    Which I do well, for I am sure the Emperor   185
    Paid ere he promis'd ; whereby his suit was granted
    Ere it was ask'd—but when the way was made,
    And pav'd with gold, the Emperor thus desir'd,
    That he would please to alter the King's course,
*   And break the foresaid peace. Let the King know,   190
    As soon he shall by me, that thus the Cardinal
    Does buy and sell his honour as he pleases,
    And for his own advantage.
NOR.   I am sorry
    To hear this of him, and could wish he were
    Something mistaken in't.
BUCK.   No, not a syllable :   195
    I do pronounce him in that very shape
    He shall appear in proof.

    Enter BRANDON, *a* Sergeant-at-Arms *before him, and two*
                or three of the Guard.

| BRAN. Your office, sergeant : execute it.
SERG.   Sir,
    My lord the Duke of Buckingham, and Earl
    Of Hereford, Stafford, and Northampton, I   200

Lines 172–174, 'But
our . . . did it',
omitted.

*Line 190, after 'the
foresaid peace':
SCENE 4
*Interior. Wolsey's
Palace. Day.*
Wolsey at work signing
papers, etc.

SCENE 5
*Interior. London. The
Royal Palace. Day.*
NORFOLK and
BUCKINGHAM walking
together.

Enter SUFFOLK,
Sergeant-at-Arms, etc.

| SUFFOLK for BRANDON
throughout.

36

Arrest thee of high treason, in the name
Of our most sovereign King.
BUCK.   Lo you, my lord,
The net has fall'n upon me !   I shall perish
Under device and practice.
| BRAN.   I am sorry | SUFFOLK for BRANDON
To see you ta'en from liberty, to look on   205   throughout.
The business present ; 'tis his Highness' pleasure
You shall to th' Tower.
BUCK.   It will help me nothing
To plead mine innocence ; for that dye is on me
Which makes my whit'st part black.   The will of heav'n
Be done in this and all things !   I obey.   210
O my Lord Aberga'ny, fare you well !
| BRAN. Nay, he must bear you company. |
[To ABERGAVENNY.]   The King
Is pleas'd you shall to th' Tower, till you know
How he determines further.
ABER.   As the Duke said,
The will of heaven be done, and the King's pleasure   215
By me obey'd.
| BRAN.   Here is warrant from |
The King t' attach Lord Montacute and the bodies
Of the Duke's confessor, John de la Car,
One Gilbert Peck, his chancellor—
BUCK.   So, so !
These are the limbs o' th' plot ; no more, I hope.   220
| BRAN. A monk o' th' Chartreux. |
BUCK.   O, Nicholas Hopkins ?
| BRAN.   He. |
BUCK. My surveyor is false.   The o'er-great Cardinal
Hath show'd him gold ; my life is spann'd already.
I am the shadow of poor Buckingham,
Whose figure even this instant cloud puts on   225
By dark'ning my clear sun.   My lord, farewell.   [Exeunt.

SCENE II.   London.   The Council Chamber.   SCENE 6
                                                       Interior. London. The
Cornets.   Enter KING HENRY, leaning on the CARDINAL'S shoulder,   Royal Palace. A
the NOBLES, and SIR THOMAS LOVELL, with Others.   The Cardinal   Chamber. Day.
places himself under the King's feet on his right side.   CROMWELL is also
                                                       among those present.
KING. My life itself, and the best heart of it,
Thanks you for this great care ; I stood i' th' level
Of a full-charg'd confederacy, and give thanks
To you that chok'd it.   Let be call'd before us
That gentleman of Buckingham's.   In person   5
I'll hear his confessions justify ;
And point by point the treasons of his master
He shall again relate.

A noise within, crying 'Room for the Queen!'   Enter the QUEEN,   GRIFFITH also
usher'd by the DUKES OF NORFOLK and SUFFOLK ; she kneels.   The   accompanies the
King riseth from his state, takes her up, kisses and placeth her by him.   QUEEN.

Q. KATH. Nay, we must longer kneel : I am a suitor.
                                                                           o

KING. Arise, and take place by us.   Half your suit   10
   Never name to us : you have half our power.
   The other moiety ere you ask is given ;
   Repeat your will, and take it.
Q. KATH.   Thank your Majesty.
   That you would love yourself, and in that love
   Not unconsidered leave your honour nor   15
   The dignity of your office, is the point
   Of my petition.
KING.   Lady mine, proceed.
Q. KATH. I am solicited, not by a few,
   And those of true condition, that your subjects
   Are in great grievance : there have been commissions   20
   Sent down among 'em which hath flaw'd the heart
   Of all their loyalties ; wherein, although,
   My good Lord Cardinal, they vent reproaches
   Most bitterly on you as putter-on
   Of these exactions, yet the King our master—   25
   Whose honour Heaven shield from soil !—even he escapes not
   Language unmannerly ; yea, such which breaks
   The sides of loyalty, and almost appears
   In loud rebellion.
NOR.   Not almost appears—
   It doth appear ; for, upon these taxations,   30
   The clothiers all, not able to maintain
   The many to them 'longing, have put off
   The spinsters, carders, fullers, weavers, who
   Unfit for other life, compell'd by hunger
   And lack of other means, in desperate manner   35
   Daring th' event to th' teeth, are all in uproar,
   And danger serves among them.
KING.   Taxation !
   Wherein ? and what taxation ?   My Lord Cardinal,
   You that are blam'd for it alike with us,
   Know you of this taxation ?
WOL.   Please you, sir,   40
   I know but of a single part in aught
   Pertains to th' state, and front but in that file
   Where others tell steps with me.
Q. KATH.   No, my lord !
   You know no more than others !   But you frame
   Things that are known alike, which are not wholesome   45
   To those which would not know them, and yet must
   Perforce be their acquaintance.   These exactions,
   Whereof my sovereign would have note, they are
   Most pestilent to th' hearing ; and to bear 'em
   The back is sacrifice to th' load.   They say   50
   They are devis'd by you, or else you suffer
   Too hard an exclamation.
KING.   Still exaction !
   The nature of it ?   In what kind, let's know,
   Is this exaction ?
Q. KATH.   I am much too venturous
   In tempting of your patience, but am bold'ned   55

Under your promis'd pardon. The subjects' grief
Comes through commissions, which compels from each
The sixth part of his substance, to be levied
Without delay ; and the pretence for this
Is nam'd your wars in France. This makes bold mouths ;   60
Tongues spit their duties out, and cold hearts freeze
Allegiance in them ; their curses now
Live where their prayers did ; and it's come to pass
This tractable obedience is a slave
To each incensed will. I would your Highness   65
Would give it quick consideration, for
There is no primer business.
KING.   By my life,
This is against our pleasure.
WOL.   And for me,
I have no further gone in this than by
A single voice ; and that not pass'd me but   70
By learned approbation of the judges. If I am
Traduc'd by ignorant tongues, which neither know
My faculties nor person, yet will be
The chronicles of my doing, let me say
'Tis but the fate of place, and the rough brake   75
That virtue must go through. We must not stint
Our necessary actions in the fear
To cope malicious censurers, which ever
As rav'nous fishes do a vessel follow
That is new-trimm'd, but benefit no further   80
Than vainly longing. What we oft do best,
By sick interpreters, once weak ones, is
Not ours, or not allow'd ; what worst, as oft
Hitting a grosser quality, is cried up
For our best act.   If we shall stand still,   85
In fear our motion will be mock'd or carp'd at,
We should take root here where we sit, or sit
State-statues only.
KING.   Things done well
And with a care exempt themselves from fear :
Things done without example, in their issue   90
Are to be fear'd. Have you a precedent
Of this commission ? I believe, not any.
We must not rend our subjects from our laws,
And stick them in our will. Sixth part of each ?
A trembling contribution ! Why, we take   95
From every tree lop, bark, and part o' th' timber ;
And though we leave it with a root, thus hack'd,
The air will drink the sap. To every county
Where this is question'd send our letters with
Free pardon to each man that has denied   100
The force of this commission. Pray, look to't ;
I put it to your care.
WOL. [*Aside to the* Secretary.] A word with you.   *Aside to* CROMWELL.
Let there be letters writ to every shire
Of the King's grace and pardon. The grieved commons
Hardly conceive of me—let it be nois'd   105

That through our intercession this revokement
And pardon comes.   I shall anon advise you
Further in the proceeding.   [*Exit* Secretary.   *Exit* CROMWELL.

Enter SURVEYOR.

Q. KATH. I am sorry that the Duke of Buckingham
   Is run in your displeasure.
KING.   It grieves many.   110
   The gentleman is learn'd and a most rare speaker ;
   To nature none more bound ; his training such
   That he may furnish and instruct great teachers
   And never seek for aid out of himself.   Yet see,
   When these so noble benefits shall prove   115
   Not well dispos'd, the mind growing once corrupt,
   They turn to vicious forms, ten times more ugly
   Than ever they were fair.   This man so complete,
   Who was enroll'd 'mongst wonders, and when we,
   Almost with ravish'd list'ning, could not find   120
   His hour of speech a minute—he, my lady,
   Hath into monstrous habits put the graces
   That once were his, and is become as black
   As if besmear'd in hell.   Sit by us ; you shall hear—
   This was his gentleman in trust—of him   125
   Things to strike honour sad.   Bid him recount
   The fore-recited practices, whereof
   We cannot feel too little, hear too much.
WOL. Stand forth, and with bold spirit relate what you,
   Most like a careful subject, have collected   130
   Out of the Duke of Buckingham.
KING.   Speak freely.
SURV. First, it was usual with him—every day
   It would infect his speech—that if the King
   Should without issue die, he'll carry it so
   To make the sceptre his.   These very words   135
   I've heard him utter to his son-in-law,
   Lord Aberga'ny, to whom by oath he menac'd
   Revenge upon the Cardinal.
WOL.   Please your Highness, note
   This dangerous conception in this point :
   Not friended by his wish, to your high person   140
   His will is most malignant, and it stretches
   Beyond you to your friends.
Q. KATH.   My learn'd Lord Cardinal,
   Deliver all with charity.
KING.   Speak on.
   How grounded he his title to the crown
   Upon our fail ?   To this point hast thou heard him   145
   At any time speak aught ?
SURV.   He was brought to this
   By a vain prophecy of Nicholas Henton.
KING. What was that Henton ?
SURV.   Sir, a Chartreux friar,
   His confessor, who fed him every minute
   With words of sovereignty.

KING.   How know'st thou this ?   150
SURV. Not long before your Highness sped to France,
　　The Duke being at the Rose, within the parish
　　Saint Lawrence Poultney, did of me demand
　　What was the speech among the Londoners
　　Concerning the French journey. I replied   155
　　Men fear'd the French would prove perfidious,
　　To the King's danger. Presently the Duke
　　Said 'twas the fear indeed and that he doubted
　　'Twould prove the verity of certain words
　　Spoke by a holy monk ' that oft ' says he   160
　　' Hath sent to me, wishing me to permit
　　John de la Car, my chaplain, a choice hour
　　To hear from him a matter of some moment ;
　　Whom after under the confession's seal
　　He solemnly had sworn that what he spoke   165
　　My chaplain to no creature living but
　　To me should utter, with demure confidence
　　This pausingly ensu'd : " Neither the King nor's heirs,
　　Tell you the Duke, shall prosper ; bid him strive
　　To gain the love o' th' commonalty ; the Duke   170
　　Shall govern England " '.
Q. KATH.   If I know you well,
　　You were the Duke's surveyor, and lost your office.
　　On the complaint o' th' tenants. Take good heed
　　You charge not in your spleen a noble person.
　　And spoil your nobler soul. I say, take heed ;   175
　　Yes, heartily beseech you.
KING.   Let him on.
　　Go forward.
SURV. On my soul, I'll speak but truth.
　　I told my lord the Duke, by th' devil's illusions
　　The monk might be deceiv'd, and that 'twas dangerous for him
　　To ruminate on this so far, until   180
　　It forg'd him some design, which, being believ'd,
　　It was much like to do. He answer'd 'Tush,
　　It can do me no damage ' ; adding further
　　That, had the King in his last sickness fail'd,
　　The Cardinal's and Sir Thomas Lovell's heads   185
　　Should have gone off.
KING.   Ha ! what, so rank ? Ah ha !
　　There's mischief in this man. Canst thou say further ?
SURV. I can, my liege.
KING.   Proceed.
SURV.   Being at Greenwich,
　　After your Highness had reprov'd the Duke
　　About Sir William Bulmer—
KING.   I remember   190
　　Of such a time : being my sworn servant,
　　The Duke retain'd him his. But on : what hence ?
SURV. ' If ' quoth he ' I for this had been committed—
　　As to the Tower I thought—I would have play'd
　　The part my father meant to act upon   195
　　Th' usurper Richard ; who, being at Salisbury,

Made suit to come in's presence, which if granted,
As he made semblance of his duty, would
Have put his knife into him.'
KING.   A giant traitor!
WOL. Now, madam, may his Highness live in freedom,   200
And this man out of prison?
Q. KATH.   God mend all!
KING. There's something more would out of thee: what say'st?
SURV. After ' the Duke his father ' with the ' knife ',
He stretch'd him, and, with one hand on his dagger,
Another spread on's breast, mounting his eyes,   205
He did discharge a horrible oath, whose tenour
Was, were he evil us'd, he would outgo
His father by as much as a performance
Does an irresolute purpose.
KING.   There's his period,
To sheath his knife in us.   He is attach'd;   210
Call him to present trial.   If he may
Find mercy in the law, 'tis his; if none,
Let him not seek't of us.   By day and night!
He's traitor to th' height.   [*Exeunt.*

SCENE III.   London.   The palace.

Enter the LORD CHAMBERLAIN and LORD SANDYS.

CHAM. Is't possible the spells of France should juggle
Men into such strange mysteries?
SANDYS.   New customs,
Though they be never so ridiculous,
Nay, let 'em be unmanly, yet are follow'd.
CHAM. As far as I see, all the good our English   5
Have got by the late voyage is but merely
A fit or two o' th' face; but they are shrewd ones;
For when they hold 'em, you would swear directly
Their very noses had been counsellors
To Pepin or Clotharius, they keep state so.   10
SANDYS. They have all new legs, and lame ones.   One would take it,
That never saw 'em pace before, the spavin
Or springhalt reign'd among 'em.
CHAM.   Death! my lord,
Their clothes are after such a pagan cut to't,
That sure th' have worn out Christendom.

Enter SIR THOMAS LOVELL.

How now?   15
What news, Sir Thomas Lovell?
LOV.   Faith, my lord,
I hear of none but the new proclamation
That's clapp'd upon the court gate.
CHAM.   What is't for?
LOV. The reformation of our travell'd gallants,
That fill the court with quarrels, talk, and tailors.   20
CHAM. I am glad 'tis there.   Now I would pray our monsieurs

SCENE 7
*Exterior. London. The
Precincts of the Royal
Palace. Day.*
LORD CHAMBERLAIN
and LORD SANDYS pass
two fantastically
dressed gentlemen.

Lines 5–13, 'reign'd
among 'em', omitted.

To think an English courtier may be wise,
And never see the Louvre.
LOV.   They must either,
    For so run the conditions, leave those remnants
    Of fool and feather that they got in France,   25
    With all their honourable points of ignorance
    Pertaining thereunto—as fights and fireworks ;
    Abusing better men than they can be,
    Out of a foreign wisdom—renouncing clean
    The faith they have in tennis, and tall stockings,   30
    Short blist'red breeches, and those types of travel,
    And understand again like honest men,
    Or pack to their old playfellows.   There, I take it,
    They may, cum privilegio, wear away
    The lag end of their lewdness and be laugh'd at.   35
SANDYS. 'Tis time to give 'em physic, their diseases
    Are grown so catching.
CHAM.   What a loss our ladies
    Will have of these trim vanities !
LOV.   Ay, marry,
    There will be woe indeed, lords : the sly whoresons
    Have got a speeding trick to lay down ladies.   40
    A French song and a fiddle has no fellow.
SANDYS. The devil fiddle 'em ! I am glad they are going,
    For sure there's no converting 'em.   Now
    An honest country lord, as I am, beaten
    A long time out of play, may bring his plainsong   45
    And have an hour of hearing ; and, by'r Lady,
    Held current music too.
CHAM.   Well said, Lord Sandys ;
    Your colt's tooth is not cast yet.
SANDYS.   No, my lord,
    Nor shall not while I have a stump.
CHAM.   Sir Thomas,
    Whither were you a-going ?
LOV.   To the Cardinal's ;   50
    Your lordship is a guest too.
CHAM.   O, 'tis true ;
    This night he makes a supper, and a great one,
    To many lords and ladies ; there will be
    The beauty of this kingdom, I'll assure you.
LOV. That churchman bears a bounteous mind indeed,   55
    A hand as fruitful as the land that feeds us ;
    His dews fall everywhere.
CHAM.   No doubt he's noble ;
    He had a black mouth that said other of him.
SANDYS. He may, my lord ; has wherewithal.   In him
    Sparing would show a worse sin than ill doctrine :   60
    Men of his way should be most liberal,
    They are set here for examples.
CHAM.   True, they are so ;
    But few now give so great ones.   My barge stays ;
    Your lordship shall along.   Come, good Sir Thomas,
    We shall be late else ; which I would not be,   65

Lines 26–32 omitted.

For I was spoke to, with Sir Henry Guildford,
This night to be comptrollers.
SANDYS. I am your lordship's. [Exeunt.

SCENE IV. *London. The Presence Chamber in York Place.*

Hautboys. A small table under a state for the Cardinal, a longer table for the guests. Then enter ANNE BULLEN, *and divers other* Ladies *and* Gentlemen, *as guests, at one door ; at another door enter* SIR HENRY GUILDFORD.

GUILD. Ladies, a general welcome from his Grace
Salutes ye all ; this night he dedicates
To fair content and you. None here, he hopes,
In all this noble bevy, has brought with her
One care abroad ; he would have all as merry
As, first, good company, good wine, good welcome,
Can make good people.

Enter LORD CHAMBERLAIN, LORD SANDYS, *and* SIR THOMAS LOVELL.

                                    O, my lord, y'are tardy,
The very thought of this fair company
Clapp'd wings to me.
CHAM. You are young, Sir Harry Guildford.
SANDYS. Sir Thomas Lovell, had the Cardinal   10
But half my lay thoughts in him, some of these
Should find a running banquet ere they rested
I think would better please 'em. By my life,
They are a sweet society of fair ones.
LOV. O that your lordship were but now confessor   15
To one or two of these !
SANDYS.   I would I were ;
They should find easy penance.
LOV.   Faith, how easy ?
SANDYS. As easy as a down bed would afford it.
CHAM. Sweet ladies, will it please you sit ? Sir Harry,
Place you that side ; I'll take the charge of this.   20
His Grace is ent'ring. Nay, you must not freeze :
Two women plac'd together makes cold weather.
My Lord Sandys, you are one will keep 'em waking :
Pray sit between these ladies.
SANDYS.   By my faith,
And thank your lordship. By your leave, sweet ladies. 25
    [*Seats himself between* ANNE BULLEN *and another lady.*
If I chance to talk a little wild, forgive me ;
I had it from my father.
ANNE.   Was he mad, sir ?
SANDYS. O, very mad, exceeding mad, in love too.
But he would bite none ; just as I do now,
He would kiss you twenty with a breath.   [*Kisses her.*
CHAM.   Well said, my lord.   30
So, now y'are fairly seated. Gentlemen,
The penance lies on you if these fair ladies
Pass away frowning.

SCENE 8
Interior. Wolsey's Palace. Night.

Lines 30–34, 'Well said . . . alone', omitted.

SANDYS.   For my little cure,
  Let me alone.

Lines 30–34 omitted.

Hautboys. Enter CARDINAL WOLSEY, *attended ; and takes his state.*

WOL. Y'are welcome, my fair guests.   That noble lady   35
  Or gentleman that is not freely merry
  Is not my friend.   This, to confirm my welcome—
  And to you all, good health !   [*Drinks.*
SANDYS.   Your Grace is noble.
  Let me have such a bowl may hold my thanks
  And save me so much talking.
WOL.   My Lord Sandys,   40
  I am beholding to you.   Cheer your neighbours.
  Ladies, you are not merry.   Gentlemen,
  Whose fault is this ?
SANDYS.   The red wine first must rise
  In their fair cheeks, my lord ; then we shall have 'em
  Talk us to silence.
ANNE.   You are a merry gamester,   45
  My Lord Sandys.
SANDYS.   Yes, if I make my play.
  Here's to your ladyship ; and pledge it, madam,
  For 'tis to such a thing—
ANNE.   You cannot show me.
SANDYS. I told your Grace they would talk anon.
         [*Drum and trumpet.   Chambers discharg'd.*
WOL.   What's that ?
CHAM. Look out there, some of ye.   [*Exit a Servant.*
WOL.   What warlike voice,   50
  And to what end, is this ?   Nay, ladies, fear not :
  By all the laws of war y'are privileg'd.

*After line 52:
SCENE 9
Exterior. Outside
Wolsey's Palace. Night.
A barge arrives at the
landing stage. The
KING steps ashore. He
and his retinue don
their masks.

Re-enter Servant.

CHAM. How now ! what is't ?
SERV.   A noble troop of strangers—
  For so they seem.   Th' have left their barge and landed,
  And hither make, as great ambassadors   55
  From foreign princes.
WOL.   Good Lord Chamberlain,
  Go, give 'em welcome ; you can speak the French tongue ;
  And pray receive 'em nobly and conduct 'em
  Into our presence, where this heaven of beauty
  Shall shine at full upon them.   Some attend him.   60
     [*Exit* CHAMBERLAIN *attended.   All rise, and tables remov'd.*
  You have now a broken banquet, but we'll mend it.
  A good digestion to you all ; and once more
  I show'r a welcome on ye ; welcome all.

SCENE 10
Interior. Wolsey's
Palace. Night.

Hautboys. Enter the KING, *and* OTHERS, *as maskers, habited like
  shepherds, usher'd by the* LORD CHAMBERLAIN.   *They pass directly
  before the Cardinal, and gracefully salute him.*

  A noble company !   What are their pleasures ?
CHAM. Because they speak no English, thus they pray'd   65
  To tell your Grace, that, having heard by fame

Of this so noble and so fair assembly
This night to meet here, they could do no less,
Out of the great respect they bear to beauty,
But leave their flocks and, under your fair conduct,   70
Crave leave to view these ladies and entreat
An hour of revels with 'em.
WOL.   Say, Lord Chamberlain,
They have done my poor house grace ; for which I pay 'em
A thousand thanks, and pray 'em take their pleasures.
         [*They choose ladies. The* KING *chooses* ANNE BULLEN.
KING. The fairest hand I ever touch'd ! O beauty,   75 | Lines 75–76,
  Till now I never knew thee !   [*Music. Dance.* | '. . . knew thee',
WOL. My lord ! | omitted.
CHAM. Your Grace ?
WOL. Pray tell 'em thus much from me :
  There should be one amongst 'em, by his person,
  More worthy this place than myself ; to whom,
  If I but knew him, with my love and duty   80
  I would surrender it.
CHAM.   I will, my lord.
                [*He whispers to the* Maskers.
WOL. What say they ?
CHAM.   Such a one, they all confess,
  There is indeed ; which they would have your Grace
  Find out, and he will take it.
WOL.   Let me see, then.   [*Comes from his state.*
  By all your good leaves, gentlemen, here I'll make   85
  My royal choice.
KING. [*Unmasking.*] Ye have found him, Cardinal.
  You hold a fair assembly ; you do well, lord.
  You are a churchman, or, I'll tell you, Cardinal,
  I should judge now unhappily.
WOL.   I am glad
  Your Grace is grown so pleasant.
KING.   My Lord Chamberlain,   90
  Prithee come hither : what fair lady's that ?
CHAM. An't please your Grace, Sir Thomas Bullen's daughter—
  The Viscount Rochford—one of her Highness' women.
KING. By heaven, she is a dainty one. Sweet heart,
  I were unmannerly to take you out   95
  And not to kiss you. A health, gentlemen !
  Let it go round.
WOL. Sir Thomas Lovell, is the banquet ready
  I' th' privy chamber ?
LOV.   Yes, my lord.
WOL.   Your Grace,
  I fear, with dancing is a little heated.   100
KING. I fear, too much.
WOL.   There's fresher air, my lord,
  In the next chamber.
KING. Lead in your ladies, ev'ry one. Sweet partner,
  I must not yet forsake you. Let's be merry :
  Good my Lord Cardinal, I have half a dozen healths   105
  To drink to these fair ladies, and a measure

To lead 'em once again ; and then let's dream
Who's best in favour.   Let the music knock it.
                      [Exeunt, with trumpets.

ACT TWO

Scene I.   *Westminster.   A street.*

Enter two Gentlemen, *at several doors.*

1 GENT. Whither away so fast ?
2 GENT.   O, God save ye !
  Ev'n to the Hall, to hear what shall become
  Of the great Duke of Buckingham.
1 GENT.   I'll save you
  That labour, sir.   All's now done but the ceremony
  Of bringing back the prisoner.
2 GENT.   Were you there ?   5
1 GENT. Yes, indeed, was I.
2 GENT. Pray, speak what has happen'd.
1 GENT. You may guess quickly what.
2 GENT.   Is he found guilty ?
1 GENT. Yes, truly is he, and condemn'd upon't.
2 GENT. I am sorry for't.
1 GENT.   So are a number more.
2 GENT. But, pray, how pass'd it ?   10
* 1 GENT. I'll tell you in a little.   The great Duke
  Came to the bar ; where to his accusations
  He pleaded still not guilty, and alleged
  Many sharp reasons to defeat the law.
  The King's attorney, on the contrary,   15
  Urg'd on the examinations, proofs, confessions,
  Of divers witnesses ; which the Duke desir'd
  To have brought, viva voce, to his face ;
  At which appear'd against him his surveyor,
  Sir Gilbert Peck his chancellor, and John Car,   20
  Confessor to him, with that devil-monk,
  Hopkins, that made this mischief.
2 GENT.   That was he
  That fed him with his prophecies?
1 GENT.   The same.
  All these accus'd him strongly, which he fain
  Would have flung from him ; but indeed he could not;   25
  And so his peers, upon this evidence,
  Have found him guilty of high treason.   Much
  He spoke, and learnedly, for life ; but all
  Was either pitied in him or forgotten.
2 GENT. After all this, how did he bear himself ?   30
1 GENT. When he was brought again to th' bar to hear
  His knell rung out, his judgment, he was stirr'd
  With such an agony he sweat extremely,
  And something spoke in choler, ill and hasty ;
  But he fell to himself again, and sweetly   35
  In all the rest show'd a most noble patience.
2 GENT. I do not think he fears death.

SCENE 11
*Interior. London. A
Tavern. Day.*
Two GENTLEMEN meet
over a drink.

*Line 11, after 'I'll
tell you in a little':
They leave the tavern
and go out into the street.*

SCENE 12
*Exterior. London. A
Street. Day.*
The two GENTLEMEN
come out of the tavern.

1 GENT.   Sure, he does not ;
    He never was so womanish ; the cause
    He may a little grieve at.
2 GENT.   Certainly
    The Cardinal is the end of this.
1 GENT.   'Tis likely,   40
    By all conjectures : first, Kildare's attainder,
    Then deputy of Ireland, who remov'd,
    Earl Surrey was sent thither, and in haste too,
    Lest he should help his father.
2 GENT.   That trick of state
    Was a deep envious one.
1 GENT.   At his return   45
    No doubt he will requite it. This is noted,
    And generally : whoever the King favours
    The Cardinal instantly will find employment,
    And far enough from court too.
2 GENT.   All the commons
    Hate him perniciously, and, o' my conscience,   50
    Wish him ten fathom deep : this Duke as much
    They love and dote on ; call him bounteous Buckingham,
    The mirror of all courtesy—

> *Enter* BUCKINGHAM *from his arraignment ;* Tip-Staves *before him ; the*
  axe with the edge towards him ; Halberds *on each side ; accom-*
  panied with SIR THOMAS LOVELL, SIR NICHOLAS VAUX, SIR WILLIAM
  SANDYS, *and* Common People, *etc.*

1 GENT.   Stay there, sir,
    And see the noble ruin'd man you speak of.
2 GENT. Let's stand close, and behold him.
BUCK. All good people,
    You that thus far have come to pity me,   56
    Hear what I say, and then go home and lose me.
    I have this day receiv'd a traitor's judgment,
    And by that name must die ; yet, heaven bear witness,
    And if I have a conscience, let it sink me   60
    Even as the axe falls, if I be not faithful !
    The law I bear no malice for my death :
    'T has done, upon the premises, but justice.
    But those that sought it I could wish more Christians.
    Be what they will, I heartily forgive 'em ;   65
    Yet let 'em look they glory not in mischief
    Nor build their evils on the graves of great men,
    For then my guiltless blood must cry against 'em.
    For further life in this world I ne'er hope
    Nor will I sue, although the King have mercies   70
    More than I dare make faults. You few that lov'd me
    And dare be bold to weep for Buckingham,
    His noble friends and fellows, whom to leave
    Is only bitter to him, only dying,
    Go with me like good angels to my end   75
    And as the long divorce of steel falls on me
    Make of your prayers one sweet sacrifice,
    And lift my soul to heaven. Lead on, a God's name.

Lines 53–54 spoken in
this scene.

SCENE 13
Exterior. London. A
Street near the River.
Day.

Lines 53–54 in
previous scene.
Line 55 omitted.

They move off to the
River.

The Duke of Buckingham (Julian Glover, bareheaded) on his way to execution, escorted by Sir Nicholas Vaux (Jack McKenzie)

Barbara Kellermann as Anne Bullen with King Henry (John Stride)

Julian Glover as the Duke of Buckingham

Peter Vaughan as Gardiner

John Rowe as Cromwell and Timothy West as Wolsey

Claire Bloom as Queen Katharine

Jeremy Kemp as the Duke of Norfolk

Barbara Kellermann as Anne Bullen

Ronald Pickup as Cranmer

Cardinal Wolsey (Timothy West) and King Henry (John Stride), with the Duke of Norfolk (Jeremy Kemp) in the background

King Henry, watched by Cranmer (Ronald Pickup), holds the infant Princess Elizabeth. Left to right behind: the Duke of Norfolk (hidden), the Lord Chamberlain (John Nettleton), the Earl of Surrey (Oliver Cotton) and Gardiner (Peter Vaughan)

LOV. I do beseech your Grace, for charity,
  If ever any malice in your heart   80
  Were hid against me, now to forgive me frankly.
BUCK. Sir Thomas Lovell, I as free forgive you
  As I would be forgiven.   I forgive all.
  There cannot be those numberless offences
   Gainst me that I cannot take peace with.   No black envy   85
  Shall mark my grave.   Commend me to his Grace ,
  And if he speak of Buckingham, pray tell him
  You met him half in heaven.   My vows and prayers
  Yet are the King's, and, till my soul forsake,
  Shall cry for blessings on him.   May he live   90
  Longer than I have time to tell his years ;
  Ever belov'd and loving may his rule be ;
  And when old time shall lead him to his end,
  Goodness and he fill up one monument !
LOV. To th' water side I must conduct your Grace   95
  Then give my charge up to Sir Nicholas Vaux,
  Who undertakes you to your end.
VAUX.   Prepare there ;
  The Duke is coming ; see the barge be ready ;
  And fit it with such furniture as suits
  The greatness of his person.
BUCK.   Nay, Sir Nicholas,   100
  Let it alone ; my state now will but mock me.
  When I came hither I was Lord High Constable
  And Duke of Buckingham ; now, poor Edward Bohun.
  Yet I am richer than my base accusers
  That never knew what truth meant ; I now seal it ;   105
  And with that blood will make 'em one day groan for't.
  My noble father, Henry of Buckingham,
  Who first rais'd head against usurping Richard,
  Flying for succour to his servant Banister,
  Being distress'd, was by that wretch betray'd   110
  And without trial fell ; God's peace be with him
  Henry the Seventh succeeding, truly pitying
  My father's loss, like a most royal prince,
  Restor'd me to my honours, and out of ruins
  Made my name once more noble.   Now his son,   115
  Henry the Eighth, life, honour, name, and all
  That made me happy, at one stroke has taken
  For ever from the world.   I had my trial,
  And must needs say a noble one ; which makes me
  A little happier than my wretched father ;   120
  Yet thus far we are one in fortunes : both
  Fell by our servants, by those men we lov'd most—
  A most unnatural and faithless service.
  Heaven has an end in all.   Yet, you that hear me,
  This from a dying man receive as certain :   125
  Where you are liberal of your loves and counsels,
  Be sure you be not loose ; for those you make friends
  And give your hearts to, when they once perceive
  The least rub in your fortunes, fall away
  Like water from ye, never found again   130

SCENE 14
Exterior. London. The
Riverside. Day.
BUCKINGHAM, LOVELL,
VAUX, SANDYS.
A Barge lies waiting.

But where they mean to sink ye.   All good people,
Pray for me !   I must now forsake ye ; the last hour
Of my long weary life is come upon me.
Farewell ;
And when you would say something that is sad,   135
Speak how I fell.   I have done ; and God forgive me !
             [Exeunt BUCKINGHAM *and* Train.

1 GENT. O, this is full of pity !   Sir, it calls,
I fear, too many curses on their heads
That were the authors.
2 GENT.   If the Duke be guiltless,
'Tis full of woe ; yet I can give you inkling   140
Of an ensuing evil, if it fall,
Greater than this.
1 GENT.   Good angels keep if from us !
What may it be ?   You do not doubt my faith, sir ?
2 GENT. This secret is so weighty, 'twill require
A strong faith to conceal it.
1 GENT.   Let me have it ;   145
I do not talk much.
2 GENT.   I am confident.
You shall, sir.   Did you not of late days hear
A buzzing of a separation
Between the King and Katharine ?
1 GENT.   Yes, but it held not ;
For when the King once heard it, out of anger   150
He sent command to the Lord Mayor straight
To stop the rumour and allay those tongues
That durst disperse it.
2 GENT.   But that slander, sir,
Is found a truth now ; for it grows again
Fresher than e'er it was, and held for certain   155
The King will venture at it.   Either the Cardinal
Or some about him near have, out of malice
To the good Queen, possess'd him with a scruple
That will undo her.   To confirm this too,
Cardinal Campeius is arriv'd and lately ;   160
As all think, for this business.
1 GENT.   'Tis the Cardinal ;
And merely to revenge him on the Emperor
For not bestowing on him at his asking
The archbishopric of Toledo, this is purpos'd.
2 GENT. I think you have hit the mark ; but is't not cruel   165
That she should feel the smart of this ?   The Cardinal
Will have his will, and she must fall.
1 GENT.   'Tis woeful.
We are too open here to argue this ;
Let's think in private more.   *[Exeunt.*

SCENE II. *London.   The palace.*
Enter the LORD CHAMBERLAIN *reading this letter.*
CHAM. ' My lord,
    The horses your lordship sent for, with all the care I had, I saw

BUCKINGHAM *is taken by
barge to his execution.*

SCENE 15
*Exterior. London. A
Street. Day.*
The two GENTLEMEN.

Lines 167, 'Tis
woeful', to 169
omitted.

SCENE 16
*Interior. London. The
Royal Palace. Day.*
LORD CHAMBERLAIN

well chosen, ridden, and furnish'd. They were young and
handsome, and of the best breed in the north. When they were
ready to set out for London, a man of my Lord Cardinal's, by
commission, and main power, took 'em from me, with this
reason : his master would be serv'd before a subject, if not before
the King ; which stopp'd our mouths, sir.'
I fear he will indeed. Well, let him have them.
He will have all, I think.

Enter to the LORD CHAMBERLAIN *the* DUKES OF NORFOLK *and*
SUFFOLK.

NOR. Well met, my Lord Chamberlain.   10
CHAM. Good day to both your Graces.
SUF. How is the King employ'd ;
CHAM.   I left him private,
Full of sad thoughts and troubles.
NOR.   What's the cause ?
CHAM. It seems the marriage with his brother's wife
Has crept too near his conscience.
SUF.   No, his conscience   15
Has crept too near another lady.
NOR.   'Tis so ;
This is the Cardinal's doing ; the King-Cardinal,
That blind priest, like the eldest son of fortune,
Turns what he list. The King will know him one day.
SUF. Pray God he do ! He'll never know himself else.   20
NOR. How holily he works in all his business !
And with what zeal ! For, now he has crack'd the league
Between us and the Emperor, the Queen's great nephew,
He dives into the King's soul and there scatters
Dangers, doubts, wringing of the conscience,   25
Fears, and despairs—and all these for his marriage ;
And out of all these to restore the King,
He counsels a divorce, a loss of her
That like a jewel has hung twenty years
About his neck, yet never lost her lustre ;   30
Of her that loves him with that excellence
That angels love good men with ; even of her
That, when the greatest stroke of fortune falls,
Will bless the King—and is not this course pious ?
CAM. Heaven keep me from such counsel ! 'Tis most true   35
These news are everywhere ; every tongue speaks 'em,
And every true heart weeps for't. All that dare
Look into these affairs see this main end—
The French King's sister. Heaven will one day open
The King's eyes, that so long have slept upon   40
This bold bad man.
SUF.   And free us from his slavery.
NOR. We had need pray, and heartily, for our deliverance ;
Or this imperious man will work us all
From princes into pages. All men's honours   45
Lie like one lump before him, to be fashion'd
Into what pitch he please.
SUF.   For me, my lords,

I love him not, nor fear him—there's my creed
As I am made without him, so I'll stand,
If the King please ; his curses and his blessings
Touch me alike ; th'are breath I not believe in.   50
I knew him, and I know him ; so I leave him
To him that made him proud—the Pope.
NOR.   Let's in ;
And with some other business put the King
From these sad thoughts that work too much upon him.
My lord, you'll bear us company ?   55
CHAM.   Excuse me,
The King has sent me otherwhere ; besides,
You'll find a most unfit time to disturb him.
Health to your lordships !
NOR. Thanks, my good Lord Chamberlain.
  [*Exit* LORD CHAMBERLAIN ; *and the* KING *draws the curtain and sits
                                            reading pensively.*
SUF. How sad he looks ; sure, he is much afflicted.
KING. Who's there, ha ?   60
NOR.   Pray God he be not angry.
K. HEN. Who's there, I say ? How dare you thrust yourselves
Into my private meditations ?
Who am I, ha ?
NOR. A gracious king that pardons all offences
Malice ne'er meant. Our breach of duty this way   65
Is business of estate, in which we come
To know your royal pleasure.
KING.   Ye are too bold.
Go to ; I'll make ye know your times of business.
Is this an hour for temporal affairs, ha ?   70

          Enter WOLSEY *and* CAMPEIUS *with a commission.*

Who's there ? My good Lord Cardinal ? O my Wolsey,
The quiet of my wounded conscience,
Thou are a cure fit for a King. [*To* CAMPEIUS.] You're welcome,
Most learned reverend sir, into our kingdom.
Use us and it. [*To* WOLSEY.] My good lord, have great care 75
I be not found a talker.
WOL.   Sir, you cannot.
I would your Grace would give us but an hour
Of private conference.
KING. [*To* NORFOLK *and* SUFFOLK.] We are busy ; go.
NOR. [*Aside to* SUFFOLK.] This priest has no pride in him !
SUF. [*Aside to* NORFOLK.] Not to speak of !
I would not be so sick though for his place.   80
But this cannot continue.
NOR. [*Aside to* SUFFOLK.] If it do,
I'll venture one have-at-him.
SUF. [*Aside to* NORFOLK.] I another.
                              [*Exeunt* NORFOLK *and* SUFFOLK.
WOL. Your Grace has given a precedent of wisdom
Above all princes, in committing freely
Your scruple to the voice of Christendom.
Who can be angry now ? What envy reach you ?   85

SCENE 17
*Interior. London. The
Royal Palace. Day.*
SUFFOLK *and* NORFOLK
enter to the KING.

The Spaniard, tied by blood and favour to her,
Must now confess, if they have any goodness,
The trial just and noble.   All the clerks,
I mean the learned ones, in Christian kingdoms   90
Have their free voices.   Rome the nurse of judgment,
Invited by your noble self, hath sent
Our general tongue unto us, this good man,
This just and learned priest, Cardinal Campeius,
Whom once more I present unto your Highness.   95
KING. And once more in mine arms I bid him welcome,
And thank the holy conclave for their loves.
They have sent me such a man I would have wish'd for.
CAM. Your Grace must needs deserve all strangers' loves,
You are so noble.   To your Highness' hand   100
I tender my commission ; by whose virtue—
The court of Rome commanding—you, my Lord
Cardinal of York, are join'd with me their servant
In the unpartial judging of this business.
KING. Two equal men.   The Queen shall be acquainted   105
Forthwith for what you come.   Where's Gardiner ?
WOL. I know your Majesty has always lov'd her
So dear in heart not to deny her that
A woman of less place might ask by law—
Scholars allow'd freely to argue for her.   110
KING. Ay ; and the best she shall have ; and my favour
To him that does best.   God forbid else.   Cardinal,
Prithee call Gardiner to me, my new secretary ;
I find him a fit fellow.   [*Exit* WOLSEY.

          Re-enter WOLSEY *with* GARDINER.

WOL. [*Aside to* GARDINER.]   Give me your hand : much joy and
favour to you ;   115
You are the King's now.
GARD. [*Aside to* WOLSEY.]   But to be commanded
For ever by your Grace, whose hand has rais'd me.
KING. Come hither, Gardiner.   [*Walks and whispers.*
CAM. My Lord of York, was not one Doctor Pace
In this man's place before him ?
WOL.   Yes, he was.   120
CAM. Was he not held a learned man ?
WOL.   Yes, surely.
CAM. Believe me, there's an ill opinion spread then,
Even of yourself, Lord Cardinal.
WOL.   How ! Of me ?
CAM. They will not stick to say you envied him
And, fearing he would rise, he was so virtuous,   125
Kept him a foreign man still ; which so griev'd him
That he ran mad and died.
WOL.   Heav'n's peace be with him !
That's Christian care enough.   For living murmurers
There's places of rebuke.   He was a fool,
For he would needs be virtuous : that good fellow,   130
If I command him, follows my appointment.
I will have none so near else.   Learn this, brother,

We live not to be grip'd by meaner persons.
KING. Deliver this with modesty to th' Queen.   [*Exit* GARDINER.
    The most convenient place that I can think of   135
    For such receipt of learning is Blackfriars ;
    There ye shall meet about this weighty business—
    My Wolsey, see it furnish'd.   O, my lord,
    Would it not grieve an able man to leave
    So sweet a bedfellow ?   But, conscience, conscience !   140
    O, 'tis a tender place ! and I must leave her.   [*Exeunt.*

SCENE III.   *London.   The palace.*

Enter ANNE BULLEN *and* AN OLD LADY.

ANNE. Not for that neither.   Here's the pang that pinches :
    His Highness having liv'd so long with her, and she
    So good a lady that no tongue could ever
    Pronounce dishonour of her—by my life,
    She never knew harm-doing—O, now, after   5
    So many courses of the sun enthroned,
    Still growing in a majesty and pomp, the which
    To leave a thousand-fold more bitter than
    'Tis sweet at first t' acquire—after this process,
    To give her the avaunt, it is a pity   10
    Would move a monster.
OLD L.   Hearts of most hard temper
    Melt and lament for her.
ANNE.   O, God's will ! much better
    She ne'er had known pomp ; though't be temporal,
    Yet, if that quarrel, fortune, do divorce
    It from the bearer, 'tis a sufferance panging   15
    As soul and body's severing.
OLD L.   Alas, poor lady !
    She's a stranger now again.
ANNE.   So much the more
    Must pity drop upon her.   Verily,
    I swear 'tis better to be lowly born
    And range with humble livers in content   20
    Than to be perk'd up in a glist'ring grief
    And wear a golden sorrow.
OLD L.   Our content
    Is our best having.
ANNE.   By my troth and maidenhead,
    I would not be a queen.
OLD L.   Beshrew me, I would,
    And venture maidenhead for't ; and so would you,   25
    For all this spice of your hypocrisy.
    You that have so fair parts of woman on you
    Have too a woman's heart, which ever yet
    Affected eminence, wealth, sovereignty ;
    Which, to say sooth, are blessings ; and which gifts,   30
    Saving your mincing, the capacity
    Of your soft cheveril conscience would receive
    If you might please to stretch it.
ANNE.   Nay, good troth.

SCENE 18
*Interior. London. The
Royal Palace. A Room
in the Queen's
Apartments. Day.*

OLD L. Yes, troth and troth.   You would not be a queen !
ANNE. No, not for all the riches under heaven.   35
OLD L. 'Tis strange : a threepence bow'd would hire me,
    Old as I am, to queen it.   But, I pray you,
    What think you of a duchess ?   Have you limbs
    To bear that load of title ?
ANNE.   No, in truth.
OLD L. Then you are weakly made.   Pluck off a little ;   40
    I would not be a young count in your way
    For more than blushing comes to.   If your back
    Cannot vouchsafe this burden, 'tis too weak
    Ever to get a boy.
ANNE.   How you do talk !
    I swear again I would not be a queen   45
    For all the world.
OLD L.   In faith, for little England
    You'd venture an emballing.   I myself
    Would for Carnarvonshire, although there long'd
    No more to th' crown but that.   Lo, who comes here ?

Enter the LORD CHAMBERLAIN.

CHAM. Good morrow, ladies.   What were't worth to know   50
    The secret of your conference ?
ANNE.   My good lord,
    Not your demand ; it values not your asking.
    Our mistress' sorrows we were pitying.
CHAM. It was a gentle business and becoming
    The action of good women ; there is hope   55
    All will be well.
ANNE.   Now, I pray God, amen !
CHAM. You bear a gentle mind, and heav'nly blessings
    Follow such creatures.   That you may, fair lady,
    Perceive I speak sincerely and high note's
    Ta'en of your many virtues, the King's Majesty   60
    Commends his good opinion of you to you, and
    Does purpose honour to you no less flowing
    Than Marchioness of Pembroke ; to which title
    A thousand pound a year, annual support,
    Out of his grace he adds.
ANNE.   I do not know   65
    What kind of my obedience I should tender ;
    More than my all is nothing, nor my prayers
    Are not words duly hallowed, nor my wishes
    More worth than empty vanities ; yet prayers and wishes
    Are all I can return.   Beseech your lordship,   70
    Vouchsafe to speak my thanks and my obedience,
    As from a blushing handmaid, to his Highness ;
    Whose health and royalty I pray for.
CHAM.   Lady,
    I shall not fail t'approve the fair conceit
    The King hath of you.   [*Aside.*]   I have perus'd her well   75
    Beauty and honour in her are so mingled
    That they have caught the King ; and who knows yet
    But from this lady may proceed a gem

To lighten all this isle ?—I'll to the King
And say I spoke with you.
ANNE.   My honour'd lord !   80
[*Exit* LORD CHAMBERLAIN.
OLD L. Why, this it is : see, see !
I have been begging sixteen years in court—
Am yet a courtier beggarly—nor could
Come pat betwixt too early and too late
For any suit of pounds ; and you, O fate !   85
A very fresh-fish here—fie, fie, fie upon
This compell'd fortune !—have your mouth fill'd up
Before you open it.
ANNE.   This is strange to me.
OLD L. How tastes it ? Is it bitter ? Forty pence, no.
There was a lady once—'tis an old story—   90
That would not be a queen, that would she not,
For all the mud in Egypt. Have you heard it ?
ANNE. Come, you are pleasant.
OLD L.   With your theme I could
O'ermount the lark. The Marchioness of Pembroke !
A thousand pounds a year for pure respect !   95
No other obligation ! By my life,
That promises moe thousands : honour's train
Is longer than his foreskirt. By this time
I know your back will bear a duchess. Say,
Are you not stronger than you were ?
ANNE.   Good lady,   100
Make yourself mirth with your particular fancy,
And leave me out on't. Would I had no being,
If this salute my blood a jot ; it faints me
To think what follows.
The Queen is comfortless, and we forgetful   105
In our long absence. Pray, do not deliver
What here y' have heard to her.
OLD L.   What do you think me ?   [*Exeunt.*

SCENE IV. *London.   A hall in Blackfriars.*

Trumpets, sennet, and cornets.   Enter two Vergers, *with short silver
wands ; next them, two* Scribes, *in the habit of doctors ; after them,
the* ARCHBISHOP OF CANTERBURY *alone ; after him, the* BISHOPS OF
LINCOLN, ELY, ROCHESTER, *and* SAINT ASAPH *; next them, with some
small distance, follows a* Gentleman *bearing the purse, with the
great seal, and a Cardinal's hat ; then two* PRIESTS, *bearing each a
silver cross ; then a* Gentleman Usher *bareheaded, accompanied
with a* Sergeant-at-arms *bearing a silver mace ; then two* Gentlemen *bearing two great silver pillars ; after them, side by side, the two*
CARDINALS, WOLSEY *and* CAMPEIUS *; two* Noblemen *with the sword
and mace.   Then enter the* KING *and* QUEEN *and their* Trains.   *The
King takes place under the cloth of state ; the two Cardinals sit
under him as judges.   The Queen takes place some distance from
the King.   The Bishops place themselves on each side the court, in
manner of a consistory ; below them the Scribes.   The* LORDS *sit*

Lines 83–85, 'nor
could . . . pounds',
omitted.

SCENE 19
*Interior. London. A
Hall in Blackfriars.
Day.*
Entry procession
omitted.

56

*next the Bishops.   The rest of the Attendants stand in convenient
order about the stage.*

WOL. Whilst our commission from Rome is read,
  Let silence be commanded.
KING.   What's the need ?
  It hath already publicly been read,
  And on all sides th' authority allow'd ;
  You may then spare that time.
WOL.   Be't so ; proceed.   5
SCRIBE. Say ' Henry King of England, come into the court '.
CRIER. Henry King of England, &c.
KING. Here.
SCRIBE. Say ' Katharine Queen of England, come into the court '.
CRIER. Katharine Queen of England, &c.   [*The* QUEEN *makes no
  answer, rises out of her chair, goes about the court, comes to the* KING,
                                    and kneels at his feet ; then speaks.
Q. KATH. Sir, I desire you do me right and justice,
  And to bestow your pity on me ; for
  I am a most poor woman and a stranger   15
  Born out of your dominions, having here
  No judge indifferent, nor no more assurance
  Of equal friendship and proceeding.   Alas, sir,
  In what have I offended you ? What cause
  Hath my behaviour given to your displeasure   20
  That thus you should proceed to put me off
  And take your good grace from me ?   Heaven witness,
  I have been to you a true and humble wife,
  At all times to your will conformable,
  Ever in fear to kindle your dislike,   25
  Yea, subject to your countenance—glad or sorry
  As I saw it inclin'd.   When was the hour
  I ever contradicted your desire
  Or made it not mine too ?   Or which of your friends
  Have I not strove to love, although I knew   30
  He were mine enemy ?   What friend of mine
  That had to him deriv'd your anger did I
  Continue in my liking ?   Nay, gave notice
  He was from thence discharg'd ?   Sir, call to mind
  That I have been your wife in this obedience   35
  Upward of twenty years, and have been blest
  With many children by you.   If, in the course
  And process of this time, you can report,
  And prove it too against mine honour, aught,
  My bond to wedlock or my love and duty,   40
  Against your sacred person, in God's name,
  Turn me away and let the foul'st contempt
  Shut door upon me, and so give me up
  To the sharp'st kind of justice.   Please you, sir,
  The King, your father, was reputed for   45
  A prince most prudent, of an excellent
  And unmatch'd wit and judgment ; Ferdinand,
  My father, King of Spain, was reckon'd one
  The wisest prince that there had reign'd by many

A year before.   It is not to be question'd   50
That they had gather'd a wise council to them
Of every realm, that did debate this business,
Who deem'd our marriage lawful.   Wherefore I humbly
Beseech you, sir, to spare me till I may
Be by my friends in Spain advis'd, whose counsel   55
I will implore.   If not, i' th' name of God,
Your pleasure be fulfill'd !
WOL.   You have here, lady,
And of your choice, these reverend fathers—men
Of singular integrity and learning,
Yea, the elect o' th' land, who are assembled   60
To plead your cause.   It shall be therefore bootless
That longer you desire the court, as well
For your own quiet as to rectify
What is unsettled in the King.
CAM.   His Grace
Hath spoken well and justly ; therefore, madam,   65
It's fit this royal session do proceed
And that, without delay, their arguments
Be now produc'd and heard.
Q. KATH.   Lord Cardinal,
To you I speak.
WOL.   Your pleasure, madam ?
Q. KATH.   Sir,
I am about to weep ; but, thinking that   70
We are a queen, or long have dream'd so, certain
The daughter of a king, my drops of tears
I'll turn to sparks of fire.
WOL.   Be patient yet.
Q. KATH. I will, when you are humble ; nay, before,
Or God will punish me.   I do believe,   75
Induc'd by potent circumstances, that
You are mine enemy, and make my challenge
You shall not be my judge ; for it is you
Have blown this coal betwixt my lord and me—
Which God's dew quench !   Therefore I say again,   80
I utterly abhor, yea, from my soul
Refuse you for my judge, whom yet once more
I hold my most malicious foe and think not
At all a friend to truth.
WOL.   I do profess
You speak not like yourself, who ever yet   85
Have stood to charity and display'd th' effects
Of disposition gentle and of wisdom
O'ertopping woman's pow'r.   Madam, you do me wrong :
I have no spleen against you, nor injustice
For you or any ; how far I have proceeded,   90
Or how far further shall, is warranted
By a commission from the Consistory,
Yea, the whole Consistory of Rome.   You charge me
That I have blown this coal : I do deny it.
The King is present ; if it be known to him   95
That I gainsay my deed, how may he wound,

And worthily, my falsehood !   Yea, as much
As you have done my truth.   If he know
That I am free of your report, he knows
I am not of your wrong.   Therefore in him   100
It lies to cure me, and the cure is to
Remove these thoughts from you ;   the which before
His Highness shall speak in, I do beseech
You, gracious madam, to unthink your speaking
And to say so no more.
Q. KATH.   My lord, my lord,   105
I am a simple woman, much too weak
T' oppose your cunning.   Y'are meek and humble-mouth'd
You sign your place and calling, in full seeming,
With meekness and humility ;   but your heart
Is cramm'd with arrogancy, spleen, and pride.   110
You have, by fortune and his Highness' favours,
Gone slightly o'er low steps, and now are mounted
Where pow'rs are your retainers, and your words,
Domestics to you, serve your will as't please
Yourself pronounce their office.   I must tell you   115
You tender more your person's honour than
Your high profession spiritual ;   that again
I do refuse you for my judge and here,
Before you all, appeal unto the Pope,
To bring my whole cause 'fore his Holiness   120
And to be judg'd by him.
                    [*She curtsies to the* KING, *and offers to depart.*
CAM.   The Queen is obstinate,
Stubborn to justice, apt to accuse it, and
Disdainful to be tried by't ;   'tis not well.
She's going away.
KING.   Call her again.   125
CRIER. Katharine Queen of England, come into the court.
GENT. USHER. Madam, you are call'd back.
Q. KATH. What need you note it ?   Pray you keep your way ;
When you are call'd, return.   Now the Lord help !
They vex me past my patience.   Pray you pass on.   130
I will not tarry ;   no, nor ever more
Upon this business my appearance make
In any of their courts.   [*Exeunt* QUEEN *and her Attendants.*
KING.   Go thy ways, Kate.
That man i' th' world who shall report he has
A better wife, let him in nought be trusted   135
For speaking false in that.   Thou art, alone—
If thy rare qualities, sweet gentleness,
Thy meekness saint-like, wife-like government,
Obeying in commanding, and thy parts
Sovereign and pious else, could speak thee out—   140
The queen of earthly queens.   She's noble born ;
And like her true nobility she has
Carried herself towards me.
WOL.   Most gracious sir,
In humblest manner I require your Highness
That it shall please you to declare in hearing   145

Of all these ears—for where I am robb'd and bound,
There must I be unloos'd, although not there
At once and fully satisfied—whether ever I
Did broach this business to your Highness, or
Laid any scruple in your way which might   150
Induce you to the question on't, or ever
Have to you, but with thanks to God for such
A royal lady, spake one the least word that might
Be to the prejudice of her present state,
Or touch of her good person ?

KING.   My Lord Cardinal,   155
I do excuse you ; yea, upon mine honour,
I free you from't.   You are not to be taught
That you have many enemies that know not
Why they are so, but, like to village curs,
Bark when their fellows do.   By some of these   160
The Queen is put in anger.   Y'are excus'd.
But will you be more justified ?   You ever
Have wish'd the sleeping of this business ; never desir'd
It to be stirr'd ; but oft have hind'red, oft,
The passages made toward it.   On my honour,   165
I speak my good Lord Cardinal to this point,
And thus far clear him.   Now, what mov'd me to't,
I will be bold with time and your attention.
Then mark th' inducement.   Thus it came—give heed to't :
My conscience first receiv'd a tenderness,   170
Scruple, and prick, on certain speeches utter'd
By th' Bishop of Bayonne, then French ambassador,
Who had been hither sent on the debating
A marriage 'twixt the Duke of Orleans and
Our daughter Mary.   I' th' progress of this business,   175
Ere a determinate resolution, he—
I mean the Bishop—did require a respite
Wherein he might the King his lord advertise
Whether our daughter were legitimate,
Respecting this our marriage with the dowager,   180
Sometimes our brother's wife.   This respite shook
The bosom of my conscience, enter'd me,
Yea, with a splitting power, and made to tremble
The region of my breast, which forc'd such way
That many maz'd considerings did throng   185
And press'd in with this caution.   First, methought
I stood not in the smile of heaven, who had
Commanded nature that my lady's womb,
If it conceiv'd a male child by me, should
Do no more offices of life to't than   190
The grave does to the dead ; for her male issue
Or died where they were made, or shortly after
This world had air'd them.   Hence I took a thought
This was a judgment on me, that my kingdom,
Well worthy the best heir o' th' world, should not   195
Be gladded in't by me.   Then follows that
I weigh'd the danger which my realms stood in
By this my issue's fail, and that gave to me

Many a groaning throe.   Thus hulling in
The wild sea of my conscience, I did steer   200
Toward this remedy, whereupon we are
Now present here together ; that's to say
I meant to rectify my conscience, which
Ithen did feel full sick, and yet not well,
By all the reverend fathers of the land   205
And doctors learn'd.   First, I began in private
With you, my Lord of Lincoln ; you remember
How under my oppression I did reek,
When I first mov'd you.
LIN.   Very well, my liege.
KING. I have spoke long ; be pleas'd yourself to say   210
How far you satisfied me.
LIN.   So please your Highness,
The question did at first so stagger me—
Bearing a state of mighty moment in't
And consequence of dread—that I committed
The daring'st counsel which I had to doubt,   215
And did entreat your Highness to this course
Which you are running here.
KING.   I then mov'd you,
My Lord of Canterbury, and got your leave
To make this present summons.   Unsolicited
I left no reverend person in this court,   220
But by particular consent proceeded
Under your hands and seals ; therefore, go on,
For no dislike i' th' world against the person
Of the good Queen, but the sharp thorny points
Of my alleged reasons, drives this forward.   225
Prove but our marriage lawful, by my life
And kingly dignity, we are contented
To wear our mortal state to come with her,
Katharine our queen, before the primest creature
That's paragon'd o' th' world.
CAM.   So please your Highness,   230
The Queen being absent, 'tis a needful fitness
That we adjourn this court till further day ;
Meanwhile must be an earnest motion
Made to the Queen to call back her appeal
She intends unto his Holiness.
KING. [Aside.]   I may perceive   235
These cardinals trifle with me.   I abhor
This dilatory sloth and tricks of Rome.
My learn'd and well-beloved servant, Cranmer,
Prithee return.   With thy approach I know
My comfort comes along.—Break up the court ;
I say, set on.   [Exeunt in manner as they enter'd.

ACT THREE

SCENE I. *London.   The Queen's apartments.*

Enter the QUEEN *and her* Women, *as at work.*

Q. KATH. Take thy lute, wench.   My soul grows sad with troubles ;
Sing and disperse 'em, if thou canst.   Leave working.

SONG.

Orpheus with his lute made trees,
And the mountain tops that freeze,
    Bow themselves when he did sing ;   5
To his music plants and flowers
Ever sprung, as sun and showers
    There had made a lasting spring.

Every thing that heard him play,
Even the billows of the sea,   10
    Hung their heads and then lay by.
In sweet music is such art,
Killing care and grief of heart
    Fall asleep or hearing die.

Enter a Gentleman.

Q. KATH. How now ?   15
GENT. An't please your Grace, the two great Cardinals
    Wait in the presence.
Q. KATH. Would they speak with me ?
GENT. They will'd me say so, madam.
Q. KATH.   Pray their Graces
    To come near. [*Exit* Gentleman.] What can be their business
    With me, a poor weak woman, fall'n from favour ?   20
    I do not like their coming. Now I think on't,
    They should be good men, their affairs as righteous ;
    But all hoods make not monks.

Enter the two Cardinals, WOLSEY *and* CAMPEIUS.

WOL. Peace to your Highness !
Q. KATH. Your Graces find me here part of a housewife ;
    I would be all, against the worst may happen.   25
    What are your pleasures with me, reverend lords ?
WOL. May it please you, noble madam, to withdraw
    Into your private chamber, we shall give you
    The full cause of our coming.
Q. KATH.   Speak it here ;
    There's nothing I have done yet, o' my conscience,   30
    Deserves a corner. Would all other women
    Could speak this with as free a soul as I do !
    My lords, I care not—so much I am happy
    Above a number—if my actions
    Were tried by ev'ry tongue, ev'ry eye saw 'em,   35
    Envy and base opinion set against 'em,
    I know my life so even. If your business

SCENE 20
Interior. London. The
Royal Palace. The
Queen's Apartments.
Day.

Enter GRIFFITH.

GRIFFITH *for*
GENTLEMAN.

Exit GRIFFITH.

Seek me out, and that way I am wife in,
Out with it boldly ; truth loves open dealing.   39
WOL. Tanta est erga te mentis integritas, regina serenissima—
Q. KATH. O, good my lord, no Latin !
I am not such a truant since my coming,
As not to know the language I have liv'd in ;   44
A strange tongue makes my cause more strange, suspicious ;
Pray speak in English. Here are some will thank you,
If you speak truth, for their poor mistress' sake :
Believe me, she has had much wrong. Lord Cardinal, | 'Believe me . . . wrong'
The willing'st sin I ever yet committed   omitted.
May be absolv'd in English.
WOL.   Noble lady,   50
I am sorry my integrity should breed,
And service to his Majesty and you,
So deep suspicion, where all faith was meant.
We come not by the way of accusation
To taint that honour every good tongue blesses,   55
Nor to betray you any way to sorrow—
You have too much, good lady ; but to know
How you stand minded in the weighty difference
Between the King and you, and to deliver,
Like free and honest men, our just opinions   60
And comforts to your cause.
CAM.   Most honour'd madam,
My Lord of York, out of his noble nature,
Zeal and obedience he still bore your Grace,
Forgetting, like a good man, your late censure
Both of his truth and him—which was too far—   65
Offers, as I do, in a sign of peace,
His service and his counsel.
| Q. KATH. [Aside.]   To betray me.— | 'To betray me'
My lords, I thank you both for your good wills ;   omitted.
Ye speak like honest men—pray God ye prove so !
But how to make ye suddenly an answer,   70
In such a point of weight, so near mine honour,
More near my life, I fear, with my weak wit,
And to such men of gravity and learning,
In truth I know not. I was set at work
Among my maids, full little, God knows, looking   75
Either for such men or such business.
For her sake that I have been—for I feel
The last fit of my greatness—good your Graces,
Let me have time and counsel for my cause.
Alas, I am a woman, friendless, hopeless !   80
WOL. Madam, you wrong the King's love with these fears
Your hopes and friends are infinite.
Q. KATH.   In England
But little for my profit ; can you think, lords,
That any Englishman dare give me counsel ?
Or be a known friend, 'gainst his Highness' pleasure—   85
Though he be grown so desperate to be honest—
And live a subject ? Nay, forsooth, my friends,
They that must weigh out my afflictions,

They that my trust must grow to, live not here
They are, as all my other comforts, far hence,   90
In mine own country, lords.
CAM.   I would your Grace
Would leave your griefs, and take my counsel.
Q. KATH.   How, sir ?
CAM. Put your main cause into the King's protection ;
He's loving and most gracious.   'Twill be much
Both for your honour better and your cause ;   95
For if the trial of the law o'ertake ye
You'll part away disgrac'd.
WOL.   He tells you rightly.
Q. KATH. Ye tell me what ye wish for both—my ruin.
Is this your Christian counsel ?   Out upon ye !
Heaven is above all yet : there sits a Judge   100
That no king can corrupt.
CAM.   Your rage mistakes us.
Q. KATH. The more shame for ye ; holy men I thought ye,
Upon my soul, two reverend cardinal virtues ;
But cardinal sins and hollow hearts I fear ye.
Mend 'em, for shame, my lords.   Is this your comfort ?   105
The cordial that ye bring a wretched lady—
A woman lost among ye, laugh'd at, scorn'd ?
I will not wish ye half my miseries :
I have more charity ; but say I warned ye.
Take heed, for heaven's sake take heed, lest at once   110
The burden of my sorrows fall upon ye.
WOL. Madam, this is a mere distraction ;
You turn the good we offer into envy.
Q. KATH. Ye turn me into nothing.   Woe upon ye,
And all such false professors ! Would you have me—   115
If you have any justice, any pity,
If ye be any thing but churchmen's habits—
Put my sick cause into his hands that hates me ?
Alas ! has banish'd me his bed already,
His love too long ago ! I am old, my lords,   120
And all the fellowship I hold now with him
Is only my obedience.   What can happen
To me above this wretchedness ?   All your studies
Make me a curse like this.
CAM.   Your fears are worse.
Q. KATH. Have I liv'd thus long—let me speak myself,   125
Since virtue finds no friends—a wife, a true one ?
A woman, I dare say without vain-glory,
Never yet branded with suspicion ?
Have I with all my full affections
Still met the King, lov'd him next heav'n, obey'd him,   130
Been, out of fondness, superstitious to him,
Almost forgot my prayers to content him,
And am I thus rewarded ?   'Tis not well, lords.
Bring me a constant woman to her husband,
One that ne'er dream'd a joy beyond his pleasure,   135
And to that woman, when she has done most,
Yet will I add an honour—a great patience.

WOL. Madam, you wander from the good we aim at.
Q. KATH. My lord, I dare not make myself so guilty,
   To give up willingly that noble title   140
   Your master wed me to : nothing but death
   Shall e'er divorce my dignities.
WOL.   Pray hear me.
Q. KATH. Would I had never trod this English earth,
   Or felt the flatteries that grow upon it !
   Ye have angels' faces, but heaven knows your hearts.   145
   What will become of me now, wretched lady ?
   I am the most unhappy woman living.
   [*To her* Women.]   Alas, poor wenches, where are now your
   fortunes ?
   Shipwreck'd upon a kingdom, where no pity,
   No friends, no hope ; no kindred weep for me ;   150
   Almost no grave allow'd me. Like the lily,
   That once was mistress of the field, and flourish'd,
   I'll hang my head and perish.
WOL.   If your Grace
   Could but be brought to know our ends are honest,
   You'd feel more comfort. Why should we, good lady,   155
   Upon what cause, wrong you ? Alas, our places,
   The way of our profession is against it ;
   We are to cure such sorrows, not to sow 'em.
   For goodness' sake, consider what you do ;
   How you may hurt yourself, ay, utterly   160
   Grow from the King's acquaintance, by this carriage.
   The hearts of princes kiss obedience,
   So much they love it ; but to stubborn spirits
   They swell and grow as terrible as storms.
   I know you have a gentle, noble temper,   165
   A soul as even as a calm. Pray think us
   Those we profess, peace-makers, friends, and servants.
CAM. Madam, you'll find it so. You wrong your virtues
   With these weak women's fears. A noble spirit,
   As yours was put into you, ever casts   170
   Such doubts as false coin from it. The King loves you
   Beware you lose it not. For us, if you please
   To trust us in your business, we are ready
   To use our utmost studies in your service.
Q. KATH. Do what ye will, my lords ; and pray forgive me   175
   If I have us'd myself unmannerly ;
   You know I am a woman, lacking wit
   To make a seemly answer to such persons.
   Pray do my service to his Majesty ;
   He has my heart yet, and shall have my prayers   180
   While I shall have my life. Come, reverend fathers,
   Bestow your counsels on me ; she now begs
   That little thought, when she set footing here,
   She should have bought her dignities so dear.   [*Exeunt.*

SCENE II. *London. The palace.*

Enter the DUKE OF NORFOLK, *the* DUKE OF SUFFOLK, *the* EARL
OF SURREY, *and the* LORD CHAMBERLAIN.

SCENE 21
*Exterior. London. The
Precincts of the Royal
Palace. Day.*

NOR. If you will now unite in your complaints
And force them with a constancy, the Cardinal
Cannot stand under them : if you omit
The offer of this time, I cannot promise
But that you shall sustain moe new disgraces   5
With these you bear already.
SUR.   I am joyful
To meet the least occasion that may give me
Remembrance of my father-in-law, the Duke,
To be reveng'd on him.
SUF.   Which of the peers
Have uncontemn'd gone by him, or at least   10
Strangely neglected ? When did he regard
The stamp of nobleness in any person
Out of himself ?
CHAM. My lords, you speak your pleasures.
What he deserves of you and me I know ;
What we can do to him—though now the time   15
Gives way to us—I much fear. If you cannot
Bar his access to th' King, never attempt
Anything on him ; for he hath a witchcraft
Over the King in's tongue.
NOR.   O, fear him not !
His spell in that is out ; the King hath found   20
Matter against him that for ever mars
The honey of his language. No, he's settled,
Not to come off, in his displeasure.
SUR.   Sir,
 I should be glad to hear such news as this
Once every hour.
NOR.   Believe it, this is true :   25
In the divorce his contrary proceedings
Are all unfolded ; wherein he appears
As I would wish mine enemy.
SUR.   How came
His practices to light ?
SUF.   Most strangely.
SUR.   O, how, how ?
SUF. The Cardinal's letters to the Pope miscarried,   30
And came to th' eye o' th' King ; wherein was read
How that the Cardinal did entreat his Holiness
To stay the judgment o' th' divorce ; for if
It did take place, ' I do ' quoth he ' perceive
My king is tangled in affection to   35
A creature of the Queen's, Lady Anne Bullen '.
SUR. Has the King this ?
SUF.   Believe it.
SUR.   Will this work ?
CHAM. The King in this perceives him how he coasts
And hedges his own way. But in this point

All his tricks founder, and he brings his physic   40
After his patient's death : the King already
Hath married the fair lady.
SUR.   Would he had !
SUF. May you be happy in your wish, my lord !
For, I profess, you have it.
S UR.   Now, all my joy
Trace the conjunction !
SUR.   My amen to't !
NOR.   All men's !   45
SUF. There's order given for her coronation ;
Marry, this is yet but young, and may be left
To some ears unrecounted.   But, my lords,
She is a gallant creature, and complete
In mind and feature.   I persuade me from her   50
Will fall some blessing to this land, which shall
In it be memoriz'd.
SUR.   But will the King
Digest this letter of the Cardinal's ?
The Lord forbid !
NOR.   Marry, amen !
SUF.   No, no ;
There be moe wasps that buzz about his nose   55
Will make this sting the sooner.   Cardinal Campeius
Is stol'n away to Rome ; hath ta'en no leave ;
Has left the cause o' th' King unhandled, and
Is posted, as the agent of our Cardinal,
To second all his plot.   I do assure you   60
The King cried ' Ha ! ' at this.
CHAM.   Now, God incense him,
And let him cry ' Ha ! ' louder !
NOR.   But, my lord,
When returns Cranmer ?
SUF. He is return'd, in his opinions ; which
Have satisfied the King for his divorce,   65
Together with all famous colleges
Almost in Christendom.   Shortly, I believe,
His second marriage shall be publish'd, and
Her coronation.   Katharine no more
Shall be call'd queen, but princess dowager   70
And widow to Prince Arthur.
NOR.   This same Cranmer's
A worthy fellow, and hath ta'en much pain
In the King's business.
SUF.   He has ; and we shall see him
For it an archbishop.
NOR.   So I hear.
SUF.   'Tis so.

Enter WOLSEY *and* CROMWELL.

The Cardinal !
NOR.   Observe, observe, he's moody.   75
WOL. The packet, Cromwell,
Gave't you the King ?

Lines 48–52, 'But, my
lords . . . memoriz'd',
omitted.

Lines 73–75, 'He has
. . . he's moody',
omitted.

SCENE 22
*Interior. London. The
Royal Palace. A
Chamber. Day.*
WOLSEY, CROMWELL.

CROM. To his own hand, in's bedchamber.
WOL. Look'd he o' th' inside of the paper?
CROM.   Presently
  He did unseal them; and the first he view'd,
  He did it with a serious mind; a heed   80
  Was in his contenance. You he bade
  Attend him here this morning.
WOL.   Is he ready
  To come abroad?
CROM.   I think by this he is.
WOL. Leave me awhile.   [*Exit* CROMWELL.
  [*Aside.*] It shall be to the Duchess of Alençon,   85
  The French King's sister; he shall marry her.
  Anne Bullen! No, I'll no Anne Bullens for him;
  There's more in't than fair visage.   Bullen!
  No, we'll no Bullens.   Speedily I wish
  To hear from Rome.   The Marchioness of Pembroke!   90   We see that NORFOLK
NOR. He's discontented.   and SUFFOLK have
SUF.   May be he hears the King   entered the room.
  Does whet his anger to him.
SUR.   Sharp enough,
  Lord, for thy justice!
WOL. [*Aside.*]   The late Queen's gentlewoman, a knight's daughter,
  To be her mistress' mistress!   The Queen's queen!   95
  This candle burns not clear.   'Tis I must snuff it;
  Then out it goes.   What though I know her virtuous
  And well deserving?   Yet I know her for
  A spleeny Lutheran; and not wholesome to
  Our cause that she should lie i' th' bosom of   100
  Our hard-rul'd King.   Again, there is sprung up
  An heretic, an arch one, Cranmer; one
  Hath crawl'd into the favour of the King,
  And is his oracle.
NOR.   He is vex'd at something.

        Enter the KING, *reading of a schedule, and* LOVELL

SUR. I would 'twere something that would fret the string, 105
  The master-cord on's heart!
SUF.   The King, the King!   KING *and* LOVELL *enter*
KING. What piles of wealth hath he accumulated   *now.*
  To his own portion!   And what expense by th' hour
  Seems to flow from him!   How, i' th' name of thrift,
  Does he rake this together?—Now, my lords,   110
  Saw you the Cardinal?
NOR.   My lord, we have
  Stood here observing him.   Some strange commotion
  Is in his brain: he bites his lip and starts,
  Stops on a sudden, looks upon the ground,
  Then lays his finger on his temple; straight   115
  Springs out into fast gait; then stops again,
  Strikes his breast hard; and anon he casts
  His eye against the moon.   In most strange postures
  We have seen him set himself.
KING.   It may well be

There is a mutiny in's mind. This morning   120
Papers of state he sent me to peruse,
As I requir'd ; and wot you what I found
There—on my conscience, put unwittingly ?
Forsooth, an inventory, thus importing
The several parcels of his plate, his treasure,   125
Rich stuffs, and ornaments of household ; which
I find at such proud rate that it outspeaks
Possession of a subject.
NOR.   It's heaven's will ;
Some spirit put this paper in the packet
To bless your eye withal.
KING.   If we did think   130
His contemplation were above the earth
And fix'd on spiritual object, he should still
Dwell in his musings ; but I am afraid
His thinkings are below the moon, not worth
His serious considering.
[_The_ KING _takes his seat and whispers_ LOVELL, _who goes to the_
                                                      CARDINAL.
WOL. Heaven forgive me !   135
Ever God bless your Highness !
KING.   Good, my lord,
You are full of heavenly stuff, and bear the inventory
Of your best graces in your mind ; the which
You were now running o'er. You have scarce time
To steal from spiritual leisure a brief span   140
To keep your earthly audit ; sure, in that
I deem you an ill husband, and am glad
To have you therein my companion.
WOL.   Sir,
For holy offices I have a time ; a time
To think upon the part of business which   145
I bear i' th' state ; and nature does require
Her times of preservation, which perforce
I, her frail son, amongst my brethren mortal,
Must give my tendance to.
KING.   You have said well.
WOL. And ever may your Highness yoke together,   150
As I will lend you cause, my doing well
With my well saying !
KING.   'Tis well said again ;
And 'tis a kind of good deed to say well ;
And yet words are no deeds. My father lov'd you :
He said he did ; and with his deed did crown   155
His word upon you. Since I had my office
I have kept you next my heart ; have not alone
Employ'd you where high profits might come home,
But par'd my present havings to bestow
My bounties upon you.
WOL. [_Aside._] What should this mean ?   160 | Lines 160–161
SUR. [_Aside._] The Lord increase this business ! | omitted.
KING.   Have I not made you
The prime man of the state ? I pray you tell me

If what I now pronounce you have found true ;
And, if you may confess it, say withal
If you are bound to us or no.   What say you ?   165
WOL. My sovereign, I confess your royal graces,
Show'r'd on me daily, have been more than could
My studied purposes requite ; which went
Beyond all man's endeavours.   My endeavours,
Have ever come too short of my desires,   170
Yet fil'd with my abilities ; mine own ends
Have been mine so that evermore they pointed
To th' good of your most sacred person and
The profit of the state.   For your great graces
Heap'd upon me, poor undeserver, I   175
Can nothing render but allegiant thanks ;
My pray'rs to heaven for you ; my loyalty,
Which ever has and ever shall be growing,
Till death, that winter, kill it.
KING.   Fairly answer'd !
A loyal and obedient subject is   180
Therein illustrated ; the honour of it
Does pay the act of it, as, i' th' contrary,
The foulness is the punishment.   I presume
That, as my hand has open'd bounty to you,
My heart dropp'd love, my pow'r rain'd honour, more   185
On you than any, so your hand and heart,
Your brain, and every function of your power,
Should, notwithstanding that your bond of duty,
As 'twere in love's particular, be more
To me, your friend, than any.
WOL.   I do profess   190
That for your Highness' good I ever labour'd
More than mine own ; that am, have, and will be—
Though all the world should crack their duty to you,
And throw it from their soul ; though perils did
Abound as thick as thought could make 'em, and   195
Appear in forms more horrid—yet my duty,
As doth a rock against the chiding flood,
Should the approach of this wild river break,
And stand unshaken yours.
KING.   'Tis nobly spoken.
Take notice, lords, he has a loyal breast,   200
For you have seen him open 't.   Read o'er this ;
                                    [*Giving him papers.*
And after, this ; and then to breakfast with
What appetite you have. [*Exit the* KING, *frowning upon the*
   CARDINAL ; *the* NOBLES *throng after him, smiling and whispering.*
WOL.   What should this mean ?
What sudden anger's this ?   How have I reap'd it ?
He parted frowning from me, as if ruin   205
Leap'd from his eyes ; so looks the chafed lion
Upon the daring hunstman that has gall'd him—
Then makes him nothing.   I must read this paper ;
I fear, the story of his anger.   'Tis so ;
This paper has undone me.   'Tis th' account   210

Of all that world of wealth I have drawn together
For mine own ends ; indeed to gain the popedom,
And fee my friends in Rome.   O negligence,
Fit for a fool to fall by !   What cross devil
Made me put this main secret in the packet   215
I sent the King ?   Is there no way to cure this ?
No new device to beat this from his brains ?
I know 'twill still him strongly ; yet I know
A way, if it take right, in spite of fortune,
Will bring me off again.   What's this ?   ' To th' Pope.'   220
The letter, as I live, with all the business
I writ to's Holiness.   Nay then, farewell !
I have touch'd the highest point of all my greatness,
And from that full meridian of my glory
I haste now to my setting.   I shall fall   225
Like a bright exhalation in the evening,
And no man see me more.

Re-enter to WOLSEY *the* DUKES OF NORFOLK *and* SUFFOLK, *the*
  EARL OF SURREY, *and the* LORD CHAMBERLAIN.

NOR. Hear the King's pleasure, Cardinal, who commands you
    To render up the great seal presently
    Into our hands, and to confine yourself   230
    To Asher House, my Lord of Winchester's,
    Till you hear further from his Highness.
WOL.   Stay :
    Where's your commission, lords ?   Words cannot carry
    Authority so weighty.
SUF.   Who dare cross 'em,
    Bearing the King's will from his mouth expressly ?   235
WOL. Till I find more than will or words to do it—
    I mean your malice—know, officious lords,
    I dare and must deny it.   Now I feel
    Of what coarse metal ye are moulded—envy ;
    How eagerly ye follow my disgraces,   240
    As if it fed ye ; and how sleek and wanton
    Ye appear in every thing may bring my ruin !
    Follow your envious courses, men of malice ;
    You have Christian warrant for 'em, and no doubt
    In time will find their fit rewards.   That seal   245
    You ask with such a violence, the King—
    Mine and your master—with his own hand gave me :
    Bade me enjoy it, with the place and honours,
    During my life ; and, to confirm his goodness,
    Tied it by letters-patents.   Now, who'll take it ?   250
SUR. The King, that gave it.
WOL.   It must be himself then.
SUR. Thou art a proud traitor, priest.
WOL.   Proud lord, thou liest.
    Within these forty hours Surrey durst better
    Have burnt that tongue than said so.
SUR.   Thy ambition,
    Thou scarlet sin, robb'd this bewailing land   255
    Of noble Buckingham, my father-in-law.

SCENE 23
Interior. London.
A Room in Wolsey's
Palace. Day.
NORFOLK, SUFFOLK,
SURREY and LORD
CHAMBERLAIN enter to
WOLSEY.

The heads of all thy brother cardinals,
With thee and all thy best parts bound together,
Weigh'd not a hair of his.   Plague of your policy!
You sent me deputy for Ireland;   260
Far from his succour, from the King, from all
That might have mercy on the fault thou gav'st him;
Whilst your great goodness, out of holy pity,
Absolv'd him with an axe.
WOL.   This, and all else
This talking lord can lay upon my credit,   265
I answer is most false.   The Duke by law
Found his deserts; how innocent I was
From any private malice in his end,
His noble jury and foul cause can witness.
If I lov'd many words, lord, I should tell you   270
You have as little honesty as honour,
That in the way of loyalty and truth   │ Lines 272–275
Toward the King, my ever royal master,   │ omitted.
Dare mate a sounder man than Surrey can be
And all that love his follies.
SUR.   By my soul,   275
Your long coat, priest, protects you; thou shouldst feel
My sword i' the life-blood of thee else.   My lords,
Can ye endure to hear this arrogance?
And from this fellow?   If we this live thus tamely,
To be thus jaded by a piece of scarlet,   280
Farewell nobility!   Let his Grace go forward
And dare us with his cap like larks.
WOL.   All goodness
Is poison to thy stomach.
SUR.   Yes, that goodness
Of gleaning all the land's wealth into one,
Into your own hands, Cardinal, by extortion;   285
The goodness of your intercepted packets
You writ to th' Pope against the King; your goodness,
Since you provoke me, shall be most notorious.
My Lord of Norfolk, as you are truly noble,
As you respect the common good, the state   290
Of our despis'd nobility, our issues,
Whom, if he live, will scarce be gentlemen—
Produce the grand sum of his sins, the articles
Collected from his life.   I'll startle you
Worse than the sacring bell, when the brown wench   295
Lay kissing in your arms, Lord Cardinal.
WOL. How much, methinks, I could despise this man,
But that I am bound in charity against it!
NOR. Those articles, my lord, are in the King's hand;
But, thus much, they are foul ones.
WOL.   So much fairer   300
And spotless shall mine innocence arise,
When the King knows my truth.
SUR.   This cannot save you.
I thank my memory I yet remember
Some of these articles; and out they shall.

Now, if you can blush and cry guilty, Cardinal,   305
  You'll show a little honesty.
WOL.   Speak on, sir ;
  I dare your worst objections.   If I blush,
  It is to see a nobleman want manners.
SUR.   I had rather want those than my head.   Have at you
  First, that without the King's assent or knowledge   310
  You wrought to be a legate ; by which power
  You maim'd the jurisdiction of all bishops.
NOR. Then, that in all you writ to Rome, or else
  To foreign princes, ' Ego et Rex meus '
  Was still inscrib'd ; in which you brought the King   315
  To be your servant.
SUF.   Then, that without the knowledge
  Either of King or Council, when you went
  Ambassador to the Emperor, you made bold
  To carry into Flanders the great seal.
SUR. Item, you sent a large commission   320
  To Gregory de Cassado, to conclude,
  Without the King's will or the state's allowance,
  A league between his Highness and Ferrara.
SUF. That out of mere ambition you have caus'd
  Your holy hat to be stamp'd on the King's coin.   325
SUR. Then, that you have sent innumerable substance,
  By what means got I leave to your own conscience,
  To furnish Rome and to prepare the ways
  You have for dignities, to the mere undoing
  Of all the kingdom.   Many more there are,   330
  Which, since they are of you, and odious,
  I will not taint my mouth with.
CHAM.   O my lord,
  Press not a falling man too far !   'Tis virtue.
  His faults lie open to the laws ; let them,
  Not you, correct him.   My heart weeps to see him   335
  So little of his great self.
SUR.   I forgive him.
SUF. Lord Cardinal, the King's further pleasure is—
  Because all those things you have done of late,
  By your power legatine within this kingdom,
  Fall into th' compass of a præmunire—   340
  That therefore such a writ be sued against you :
  To forfeit all your goods, lands, tenements,
  Chattels, and whatsoever, and to be
  Out of the King's protection.   This is my charge.
NOR. And so we'll leave you to your meditations   345
  How to live better.   For your stubborn answer
  About the giving back the great seal to us,
  The King shall know it, and, no doubt, shall thank you.
  So fare you well, my little good Lord Cardinal.
                    [*Exeunt all but* WOLSEY.
WOL. So farewell to the little good you bear me.   350
  Farewell, a long farewell, to all my greatness !
  This is the state of man : to-day he puts forth
  The tender leaves of hopes ; to-morrow blossoms

And bears his blushing honours thick upon him;
The third day comes a frost, a killing frost,   355
And when he thinks, good easy man, full surely
His greatness is a-ripening, nips his root,
And then he falls, as I do. I have ventur'd,
Like little wanton boys that swim on bladders,
This many summers in a sea of glory;   360
But far beyond my depth. My high-blown pride
At length broke under me, and now has left me,
Weary and old with service, to the mercy
Of a rude stream, that must for ever hide me.
Vain pomp and glory of this world, I hate ye;   365
I feel my heart new open'd. O, how wretched
Is that poor man that hangs on princes' favours!
There is betwixt that smile we would aspire to,
That sweet aspect of princes, and their ruin
More pangs and fears than wars or women have;   370
And when he falls, he falls like Lucifer,
Never to hope again.

Enter CROMWELL, standing amazed.

                        Why, how now, Cromwell!
CROM. I have no power to speak, sir.
WOL.   What, amaz'd
At my misfortunes? Can thy spirit wonder
A great man should decline? Nay, an you weep,   375
I am fall'n indeed.
CROM. How does your Grace?
WOL.   Why, well;
Never so truly happy, my good Cromwell.
I know myself now, and I feel within me
A peace above all earthly dignities,
A still and quiet conscience. The King has cur'd me,   380
I humbly thank his Grace; and from these shoulders,
These ruin'd pillars, out of pity, taken
A load would sink a navy—too much honour.
O, 'tis a burden, Cromwell, 'tis a burden
Too heavy for a man that hopes for heaven!   385
CROM. I am glad your Grace has made that right use of it.
WOL. I hope I have. I am able now, methinks,
Out of a fortitude of soul I feel,
To endure more miseries and greater far
Than my weak-hearted enemies dare offer.   390
What news abroad?
CROM.   The heaviest and the worst
Is your displeasure with the King.
WOL.   God bless him!
CROM. The next is that Sir Thomas More is chosen
Lord Chancellor in your place.
WOL.   That's somewhat sudden.
But he's a learned man. May he continue   395
Long in his Highness' favour, and do justice
For truth's sake and his conscience; that his bones,

SCENE 24
*Interior. An Abbey in
the Country. Day.*
CROMWELL *enters to*
WOLSEY.

When he has run his course and sleeps in blessings,
May have a tomb of orphans' tears wept on him !
What more ?
CROM. That Cranmer is return'd with welcome,   400
Install'd Lord Archbishop of Canterbury.
WOL. That's news indeed.
CROM.   Last, that the Lady Anne,
Whom the King hath in secrecy long married,
This day was view'd in open as his queen,
Going to chapel ; and the voice is now   405
Only about her coronation.
WOL. There was the weight that pull'd me down.   O Cromwell,
The King has gone beyond me.   All my glories
In that one woman I have lost for ever.
No sun shall ever usher forth mine honours,   410
Or gild again the noble troops that waited
Upon my smiles.   Go get thee from me, Cromwell ;
I am a poor fall'n man, unworthy now
To be thy lord and master.   Seek the King ;
That sun, I pray, may never set !   I have told him   415
What and how true thou art.   He will advance thee ;
Some little memory of me will stir him—
I know his noble nature—not to let
Thy hopeful service perish too.   Good Cromwell,
Neglect him not ; make use now, and provide   420
For thine own future safety.
CROM.   O my lord,
Must I then leave you ?   Must I needs forgo
So good, so noble, and so true a master ?
Bear witness, all that have not hearts of iron,
With what a sorrow Cromwell leaves his lord.   425
The King shall have my service ; but my prayers
For ever and for ever shall be yours.
WOL. Cromwell, I did not think to shed a tear
In all my miseries ; but thou hast forc'd me,
Out of thy honest truth, to play the woman.   430
Let's dry our eyes ; and thus far hear me, Cromwell,
And when I am forgotten, as I shall be,
And sleep in dull cold marble, where no mention
Of me more must be heard of, say I taught thee—
Say Wolsey, that once trod the ways of glory,   435
And sounded all the depths and shoals of honour,
Found thee a way, out of his wreck, to rise in—
A sure and safe one, though thy master miss'd it.
Mark but my fall and that that ruin'd me.
Cromwell, I charge thee, fling away ambition :   440
By that sin fell the angels.   How can man then,
The image of his Maker, hope to win by it ?
Love thyself last ; cherish those hearts that hate thee ;
Corruption wins not more than honesty.
Still in thy right hand carry gentle peace   445
To silence envious tongues.   Be just, and fear not ;
Let all the ends thou aim'st at be thy country's,
Thy God's, and truth's ; then, if thou fall'st, O Cromwell,

Thou fall'st a blessed martyr !
Serve the King, and—prithee lead me in.   450
There take an inventory of all I have
To the last penny ; 'tis the King's.   My robe,
And my integrity to heaven, is all
I dare now call mine own.   O Cromwell, Cromwell!
Had I but serv'd my God with half the zeal   455
I serv'd my King, he would not in mine age
Have left me naked to mine enemies.
* CROM. Good sir, have patience.
WOL.   So I have.   Farewell
The hopes of court !   My hopes in heaven do dwell.   [*Exeunt.*

*At end of scene:
SCENE 25
*Interior. London. The
Royal Palace. Day.*
ANNE BULLEN
preparing for her
coronation.

ACT FOUR

SCENE I.   *A street in Westminster.*

Enter two Gentlemen, *meeting one another.*

SCENE 26
*Exterior. London.
A Street outside
Westminster Abbey.
Day.*
The two GENTLEMEN.

1 GENT. Y'are well met once again.
2 GENT.   So are you.
1 GENT. You come to take your stand here, and behold
The Lady Anne pass from her coronation ?
2 GENT. 'Tis all my business.   At our last encounter
The Duke of Buckingham came from his trial.   5
1 GENT. 'Tis very true.   But that time offer'd sorrow ;
This, general joy.
2 GENT.   'Tis well.   The citizens,
I am sure, have shown at full their royal minds—
As, let 'em have their rights, they are ever forward—
In celebration of this day with shows,   10
Pageants, and sights of honour.
1 GENT.   Never greater,
Nor, I'll assure you, better taken, sir.
2 GENT. May I be bold to ask what that contains,
That paper in your hand ?
1 GENT.   Yes ; 'tis the list
Of those that claim their offices this day,   15
By custom of the coronation.
The Duke of Suffolk is the first, and claims
To be High Steward ; next, the Duke of Norfolk,
He to be Earl Marshal.   You may read the rest.
2 GENT. I thank you, sir ; had I not known those customs,   20
I should have been beholding to your paper.
But, I beseech you, what's become of Katharine,
The Princess Dowager ?   How goes her business ?
1 GENT. That I can tell you too.   The Archbishop
Of Canterbury, accompanied with other   25
Learned and reverend fathers of his order,
Held a late court at Dunstable, six miles off
From Ampthill, where the Princess lay ; to which
She was often cited by them, but appear'd not.
And, to be short, for not appearance and   30
The King's late scruple, by the main assent
Of all these learned men, she was divorc'd,

And the late marriage made of none effect ;
Since which she was removed to Kimbolton,
Where she remains now sick.
2 GENT.   Alas, good lady !   [*Trumpets.*
The trumpets sound.   Stand close, the Queen is coming.   36
                                                        [*Hautboys.*

THE ORDER OF THE CORONATION.   The Coronation
                                                Procession emerges
1. *A lively flourish of trumpets.*   from the doors of the
2. *Then two* JUDGES.   Abbey.
3. LORD CHANCELLOR, *with purse and mace before him.*
4. CHORISTERS *singing.*   [*Music.*
5. MAYOR OF LONDON, *bearing the mace.   Then* GARTER, *in his coat of
   arms, and on his head he wore a gilt copper crown.*
6. MARQUIS DORSET, *bearing a sceptre of gold, on his head a demi-coronal
   of gold.   With him, the* EARL OF SURREY, *bearing the rod of silver
   with the dove, crowned with an earl's coronet.   Collars of Esses.*
7. DUKE OF SUFFOLK, *in his robe of estate, his coronet on his head, bearing
   a long white wand, as High Steward.   With him, the* DUKE OF
   NORFOLK, *with the rod of marshalship, a coronet on his head.   Collars
   of Esses.*
8. *A canopy borne by four of the* CINQUE-PORTS ; *under it the* QUEEN
   *in her robe ; in her hair richly adorned with pearl, crowned.   On
   each side her, the* BISHOPS OF LONDON *and* WINCHESTER.
9. *The old* DUCHESS OF NORFOLK, *in a coronal of gold, wrought with
   flowers, bearing the Queen's train.*
10. *Certain* LADIES *or* COUNTESSES, *with plain circlets of gold without
    flowers.*

                            [*Exeunt, first passing over the stage in
                             order and state, and then a great
                             flourish of trumpets.*

2 GENT. A royal train, believe me.   These I know.   Lines 37–55 are spoken
   Who's that that bears the sceptre ?   as the two GENTLEMEN
1 GENT.   Marquis Dorset ;   watch the Coronation
   And that the Earl of Surrey, with the rod.   Procession passing in
2 GENT. A bold brave gentleman.   That should be   40 front of them.
   The Duke of Suffolk ?
1 GENT. 'Tis the same—High Steward.
2 GENT. And that my Lord of Norfolk ?
1 GENT.   Yes.
2 GENT. [*Looking on the* QUEEN.]   Heaven bless thee !
   Thou hast the sweetest face I ever look'd on.
   Sir, as I have a soul, she is an angel ;
   Our king has all the Indies in his arms,   45
   And more and richer, when he strains that lady ;
   I cannot blame his conscience.
1 GENT.   They that bear
   The cloth of honour over her are four barons
   Of the Cinque-ports.
2 GENT. Those men are happy ; and so are all are near her. 50
   I take it she that carries up the train
   Is that old noble lady, Duchess of Norfolk.
1 GENT. It is ; and all the rest are countesses.

                                77

The Coronation Procession

Anne Bullen (Barbara Kellermann) is crowned Queen by Cranmer (Ronald Pickup)

78

2 GENT. Their coronets say so.   These are stars indeed,
     And sometimes falling ones.
1 GENT.   No more of that.   [*Exit Procession,*
                                          with a great flourish of trumpets.

                    Enter a third Gentleman.

     God save you, sir !   Where have you been broiling ?
3 GENT. Among the crowds i' th' Abbey, where a finger
     Could not be wedg'd in more ;   I am stifled
     With the mere rankness of their joy.
2 GENT.   You saw
     The ceremony ?
3 GENT.   That I did.
1 GENT.   How was it ?   60
3 GENT. Well worth the seeing.
2 GENT.   Good sir, speak it to us.
3 GENT. As well as I am able.   The rich stream
     Of lords and ladies, having brought the Queen
     To a prepar'd place in the choir, fell off
     A distance from her, while her Grace sat down   65
     To rest awhile, some half an hour or so,
     In a rich chair of state, opposing freely
     The beauty of her person to the people.
     Believe me, sir, she is the goodliest woman
     That ever lay by man ;   which when the people   70
     Had the full view of, such a noise arose
     As the shrouds make at sea in a stiff tempest,
     As loud, and to as many tunes ;   hats, cloaks—
     Doublets, I think—flew up, and had their faces
     Been loose, this day they had been lost.   Such joy   75
     I never saw before.   Great-bellied women,
     That had not half a week to go, like rams
     In the old time of war, would shake the press,
     And make 'em reel before 'em.   No man living
     Could say ' This is my wife ' there, all were woven   80
     So strangely in one piece.
2 GENT.   But what follow'd ?
3 GENT. At length her Grace rose, and with modest paces
     Came to the altar, where she kneel'd, and saintlike
     Cast her fair eyes to heaven, and pray'd devoutly.
     Then rose again, and bow'd her to the people ;   85
     When by the Archbishop of Canterbury
     She had all the royal makings of a queen :
     As holy oil, Edward Confessor's crown,
     The rod, and bird of peace, and all such emblems
     Laid nobly on her ;   which perform'd, the choir,   90
     With all the choicest music of the kingdom,
     Together sung ' Te Deum '.   So she parted,
     And with the same full state pac'd back again
     To York Place, where the feast is held.
1 GENT.   Sir,
     You must no more call it York Place : that's past   95
     For since the Cardinal fell that title's lost.
     'Tis now the King's, and call'd Whitehall.

SCENE 27
Interior. London.
Westminster Abbey.
Day.
ANNE BULLEN is
crowned Queen.
Procession omitted.
Lines 56–117 omitted.

3 GENT.   I know it ;
But 'tis so lately alter'd that the old name
Is fresh about me.
2 GENT.   What two reverend bishops
Were those that went on each side of the Queen ?   100
3 GENT. Stokesly and Gardiner : the one of Winchester,
Newly preferr'd from the King's secretary ;
The other, London.
2 GENT.   He of Winchester
Is held no great good lover of the Archbishop's,
The virtuous Cranmer.
3 GENT.   All the land knows that ;   105
However, yet there is no great breach.   When it comes,
Cranmer will find a friend will not shrink from him.
2 GENT. Who may that be, I pray you ?
3 GENT.   Thomas Cromwell,
A man in much esteem with th' King, and truly
A worthy friend.   The King has made him Master   110
O' th' Jewel House,
And one, already, of the Privy Council.
2 GENT. He will deserve more.
3 GENT.   Yes, without all doubt.
Come, gentlemen, ye shall go my way, which
Is to th' court, and there ye shall be my guests :   115
Something I can command.   As I walk thither,
I'll tell ye more.
BOTH.   You may command us, sir.   [*Exeunt.*

Lines 56–117 omitted.

SCENE II.   *Kimbolton.*

Enter KATHARINE, *Dowager, sick ; led between* GRIFFITH,
her Gentleman Usher, and PATIENCE, *her woman.*

GRIF. How does your Grace ?
KATH.   O Griffith, sick to death !
My legs like loaden branches bow to th' earth,
Willing to leave their burden.   Reach a chair.
So—now, methinks, I feel a little ease.
Didst thou not tell me, Griffith, as thou led'st me,   5
That the great child of honour, Cardinal Wolsey,
Was dead ?
GRIF. Yes, madam ; but I think your Grace,
Out of the pain you suffer'd, gave no ear to't.
KATH. Prithee, good Griffith, tell me how he died.
If well, he stepp'd before me, happily,   10
For my example.
GRIF.   Well, the voice goes, madam ;
For after the stout Earl Northumberland
Arrested him at York and brought him forward,
As a man sorely tainted, to his answer,
He fell sick suddenly, and grew so ill   15
He could not sit his mule.
KATH.   Alas, poor man !
GRIF. At last, with easy roads, he came to Leicester,
Lodg'd in the abbey ; where the reverend abbot,

SCENE 28
Interior. Kimbolton.
Katharine's Bedroom.
Night.

With all his covent, honourably receiv'd him ;
To whom he gave these words : ' O father Abbot,   20
An old man, broken with the storms of state,
Is come to lay his weary bones among ye ;
Give him a little earth for charity ! '
So went to bed ; where eagerly his sickness
Pursu'd him still. And three nights after this,   25
About the hour of eight—which he himself
Foretold should be his last—full of repentance,
Continual meditations, tears, and sorrows,
He gave his honours to the world again,
His blessed part to heaven, and slept in peace.   30
KATH. So may he rest ; his faults lie gently on him !
Yet thus far, Griffith, give me leave to speak him,
And yet with charity.   He was a man
Of an unbounded stomach, ever ranking
Himself with princes ; one that, by suggestion,   35
Tied all the kingdom.   Simony was fair play ;
His own opinion was his law.   I' th' presence
He would say untruths, and be ever double
Both in his words and meaning.   He was never,
But where he meant to ruin, pitiful.   40
His promises were, as he then was, mighty ;
But his performance, as he is now, nothing.
Of his own body he was ill, and gave
The clergy ill example.
GRIF.   Noble madam,
Men's evil manners live in brass : their virtues   45
We write in water.   May it please your Highness
To hear me speak his good now ?
KATH.   Yes, good Griffith ;
I were malicious else.
GRIF.   This Cardinal,   50
Though from an humble stock, undoubtedly
Was fashion'd to much honour from his cradle.
He was a scholar, and a ripe and good one ;
Exceeding wise, fair-spoken, and persuading ;
Lofty and sour to them that lov'd him not,
But to those men that sought him sweet as summer.
And though he were unsatisfied in getting—   55
Which was a sin—yet in bestowing, madam,
He was most princely : ever witness for him
Those twins of learning that he rais'd in you,
Ipswich and Oxford !   One of which fell with him,
Unwilling to outlive the good that did it ;   60
The other, though unfinish'd, yet so famous,
So excellent in art, and still so rising,
That Christendom shall ever speak his virtue.
His overthrow heap'd happiness upon him ;
For then, and not till then, he felt himself,   65
And found the blessedness of being little.
And, to add greater honours to his age
Than man could give him, he died fearing God.
KATH. After my death I wish no other herald,

Lines 20–25, '. . .
Pursu'd him still',
omitted.

Lines 27–28, 'full of
. . . sorrows', omitted.

Lines 43–44, '. . . ill
example', omitted.

Lines 55–63 omitted.

Oliver Cotton as the Earl of Surrey, Jeremy Kemp as the Duke of Norfolk, and Lewis Fiander as the Duke of Suffolk

Sally Home as Patience, Claire Bloom as Queen Katharine, and John Bailey as Griffith

King Henry (John Stride) with Cranmer (Ronald Pickup)

No other speaker of my living actions,   70
To keep mine honour from corruption,
But such an honest chronicler as Griffith.
Whom I most hated living, thou hast made me,
With thy religious truth and modesty,
Now in his ashes honour.   Peace be with him!   75
Patience, be near me still, and set me lower :
I have not long to trouble thee.   Good Griffith,
Cause the musicians play me that sad note
I nam'd my knell, whilst I sit meditating
On that celestial harmony I go to.   [Sad and solemn music.
GRIF. She is asleep.   Good wench, let's sit down quiet,
For fear we wake her.   Softly, gentle Patience.   82

THE VISION.

Enter, solemnly tripping one after another, six PERSONAGES *clad in white
robes, wearing on their heads garlands of bays, and golden vizards on
their faces ; branches of bays or palm in their hands.   They first
congee unto her, then dance ;   and, at certain changes, the first two
hold a spare garland over her head, at which the other four make
reverent curtsies.   Then the two that held the garland deliver the
same to the other next two, who observe the same order in their changes,
and holding the garland over her head ;   which done, they deliver
the same garland to the last two, who likewise observe the same order ;
at which, as it were by inspiration, she makes in her sleep signs of
rejoicing, and holdeth up her hands to heaven.   And so in their
dancing vanish, carrying the garland with them.   The music
continues.*

KATH. Spirits of peace, where are ye ?   Are ye all gone ?
   And leave me here in wretchedness behind ye ?
GRIF. Madam, we are here.
KATH.   It is not you I call for.   85
   Saw ye none enter since I slept ?
GRIF.   None, madam.
KATH. No ?   Saw you not, even now, a blessed troop
   Invite me to a banquet ;   whose bright faces
   Cast thousand beams upon me, like the sun ?
   They promis'd me eternal happiness,   90
   And brought me garlands, Griffith, which I feel
   I am not worthy yet to wear.   I shall, assuredly.
GRIF. I am most joyful, madam, such good dreams
   Possess your fancy.
KATH.   Bid the music leave,
   They are harsh and heavy to me.   [Music ceases.
PAT.   Do you note   95
   How much her Grace is alter'd on the sudden ?
   How long her face is drawn !   How pale she looks,
   And of an earthly cold !   Mark her eyes.
GRIF. She is going, wench.   Pray, pray.
PAT.   Heaven comfort her !

Enter a Messenger.

MESS. An't like your Grace—

SCENE 29
*Interior. Kimbolton.
Katharine's Bedroom.
Night.*
KATHARINE has a
vision.

SCENE 30
*Interior. Kimbolton.
Katharine's Bedroom.
Night.*
KATHARINE, GRIFFITH,
PATIENCE.

KATH.   You are a saucy fellow.   100
Deserve we no more reverence ?
GRIF.   You are to blame,
Knowing she will not lose her wonted greatness,
To use so rude behaviour.   Go to, kneel.
MESS. I humbly do entreat your Highness' pardon ;
My haste made me unmannerly.   There is staying   105
A gentleman, sent from the King, to see you.
KATH. Admit him entrance, Griffith ; but this fellow
Let me ne'er see again.   [*Exit* Messenger.

          Enter LORD CAPUCIUS.

                    If my sight fail not,
You should be Lord Ambassador from the Emperor,
My royal nephew, and your name Capucius.   110
CAP. Madam, the same—your servant.
KATH.   O, my Lord,
The times and titles now are alter'd strangely
With me since first you knew me.   But, I pray you,
What is your pleasure with me ?
CAP.   Noble lady,
First, mine own service to your Grace ; the next,   115
The King's request that I would visit you,
Who grieves much for your weakness, and by me
Sends you his princely commendations
And heartily entreats you take good comfort.
KATH. O my good lord, that comfort comes too late,   120
'Tis like a pardon after execution :
That gentle physic, given in time, had cur'd me ;
But now I am past all comforts here, but prayers.
How does his Highness ?
CAP.   Madam, in good health.
KATH. So may he ever do ! and ever flourish   125
When I shall dwell with worms, and my poor name
Banish'd the kingdom !   Patience, is that letter
I caus'd you write yet sent away ?
PAT.   No, madam.   [*Giving it to* KATHARINE.
KATH. Sir, I most humbly pray you to deliver
This to my lord the King.
CAP.   Most willing, madam.   130
KATH. In which I have commended to his goodness
The model of our chaste loves, his young daughter—
The dews of heaven fall thick in blessings on her .—
Beseeching him to give her virtuous breeding—
She is young, and of a noble modest nature ;   135
I hope she will deserve well—and a little
To love her for her mother's sake, that lov'd him,
Heaven knows how dearly.   My next poor petition
Is that his noble Grace would have some pity
Upon my wretched women that so long   140
Have follow'd both my fortunes faithfully ;
Of which there is not one, I dare avow—
And now I should not lie—but will deserve,
For virtue and true beauty of the soul,

For honesty and decent carriage,   145
A right good husband, let him be a noble ;
And sure those men are happy that shall have 'em.
The last is for my men—they are the poorest,
But poverty could never draw 'em from me—
That they may have their wages duly paid 'em,   150
And something over to remember me by.
If heaven had pleas'd to have given me longer life
And able means, we had not parted thus.
These are the whole contents ; and, good my lord,
By that you love the dearest in this world,   155
As you wish Christian peace to souls departed,
Stand these poor people's friend, and urge the King
To do me this last right.
CAP.   By heaven, I will,
Or let me lose the fashion of a man !
KATH. I thank you, honest lord.   Remember me   160
In all humility unto his Highness ;
Say his long trouble now is passing
Out of this world.   Tell him in death I bless'd him,
For so I will.   Mine eyes grow dim.   Farewell,
My lord.   Griffith, farewell.   Nay, Patience,   165
You must not leave me yet.   I must to bed ;
Call in more women.   When I am dead, good wench,
Let me be us'd with honour ; strew me over
With maiden flowers, that all the world may know
I was a chaste wife to my grave.   Embalm me,   170
Then lay me forth ; although unqueen'd, yet like
A queen, and daughter to a king, inter me.
* I can no more.   [*Exeunt, leading* KATHARINE.

*At end of scene:
SCENE 31
*Interior. Kimbolton.
Katharine's Bedroom.
Night.*
KATHARINE lying dead.

ACT FIVE

SCENE I.   *London.   A gallery in the palace.*

Enter GARDINER, BISHOP OF WINCHESTER, *a* Page *with a torch
before him, met by* SIR THOMAS LOVELL.

GAR. It's one o'clock, boy, is't not ?
BOY.   It hath struck.
GAR. These should be hours for necessities,
   Not for delights ; times to repair our nature
   With comforting repose, and not for us
   To waste these times.   Good hour of night, Sir Thomas !   5
   Whither so late ?
LOV. Came you from the King, my lord ?
GAR. I did, Sir Thomas, and left him at primero
   With the Duke of Suffolk.
LOV.   I must to him too,
   Before he go to bed.   I'll take my leave.
GAR. Not yet, Sir Thomas Lovell.   What's the matter ?   10
   It seems you are in haste.   An if there be
   No great offence belongs to't, give your friend
   Some touch of your late business.   Affairs that walk—
   As they say spirits do—at midnight, have

SCENE 32
*Exterior. London. The
Precincts of the Royal
Palace. Night.*

In them a wilder nature than the business   15
That seeks dispatch by day.
LOV.   My lord, I love you ;
And durst commend a secret to your ear
Much weightier than this work.   The Queen's in labour,
They say in great extremity, and fear'd
She'll with the labour end.
GAR.   The fruit she goes with   20
I pray for heartily, that it may find
Good time, and live ; but for the stock, Sir Thomas,
I wish it grubb'd up now.
LOV.   Methinks I could
Cry thee amen ; and yet my conscience says
She's a good creature, and, sweet lady, does   25
Deserve our better wishes.
GAR.   But, sir, sir—
Hear me, Sir Thomas.   Y'are a gentleman
Of mine own way ; I know you wise, religious ;
And, let me tell you, it will ne'er be well—
'Twill not, Sir Thomas Lovell, take't of me—   30
Till Cranmer, Cromwell, her two hands, and she,
Sleep in their graves.
LOV.   Now, sir, you speak of two
The most remark'd i' th' kingdom.   As for Cromwell,
Beside that of the Jewel House, is made Master
O' th' Rolls, and the King's secretary ; further, sir,   35
Stands in the gap and trade of moe preferments,
With which the time will load him.   Th' Archbishop
Is the King's hand and tongue, and who dare speak
One syllable against him ?
GAR.   Yes, yes, Sir Thomas,
There are that dare ; and I myself have ventur'd   40
To speak my mind of him ; and indeed this day,
Sir—I may tell it you—I think I have
Incens'd the lords o' th' Council, that he is—
For so I know he is, they know he is—
A most arch heretic, a pestilence   45
That does infect the land ; with which they moved
Have broken with the King, who hath so far
Given ear to our complaint—of his great grace
And princely care, foreseeing those fell mischiefs
Our reasons laid before him—hath commanded   50
To-morrow morning to the Council board
He be convented.   He's a rank weed, Sir Thomas,
And we must root him out.   From your affairs
I hinder you too long—good night, Sir Thomas.
LOV. Many good nights, my lord ; I rest your servant.   55
                              [*Exeunt* GARDINER *and* Page.

Enter the KING *and the* DUKE OF SUFFOLK.

KING. Charles, I will play no more to-night ;
   My mind's not on't ; you are too hard for me.
SUF. Sir, I did never win of you before.
KING. But little, Charles ;

SCENE 33
*Interior. London. The
Royal Palace. The
King's Private
Chamber. Night.*

Nor shall not, when my fancy's on my play.   60   LOVELL *enters*.
Now, Lovell, from the Queen what is the news?
LOV. I could not personally deliver to her
What you commanded me, but by her woman
I sent your message; who return'd her thanks
In the great'st humbleness, and desir'd your Highness   65
Most heartily to pray for her.
KING.   What say'st thou, ha?
To pray for her? What, is she crying out?
LOV. So said her woman; and that her suff'rance made
Almost each pang a death.
KING.   Alas, good lady!
SUF. God safely quit her of her burden, and   70
With gentle travail, to the gladding of
Your Highness with an heir!
KING.   'Tis midnight, Charles;
Prithee to bed; and in thy pray'rs remember
Th' estate of my poor queen. Leave me alone,
For I must think of that which company   75
Will not be friendly to.
SUF.   I wish your Highness
A quiet night, and my good mistress will
Remember in my prayers.
KING.   Charles, good night. [*Exit* SUFFOLK.

                  Enter SIR ANTHONY DENNY.   *Enter* SIR HENRY
                                                                   GUILDFORD.
Well, sir, what follows?
DEN. Sir, I have brought my lord the Archbishop.   80   GUILDFORD for DENNY
As you commanded me.   throughout.
KING.   Ha! Canterbury?
DEN. Ay, my good lord.
KING.   'Tis true. Where is he, Denny?   Guildford for Denny.
DEN. He attends your Highness' pleasure.
KING.   Bring him to us.   [*Exit* DENNY.
LOV. [*Aside*.] This is about that which the bishop spake. | Lines 84–85 omitted.
I am happily come hither.   85 |

                  Re-enter DENNY, *with* CRANMER.

KING. Avoid the gallery.   [LOVELL *seems to stay*.
                  Ha! I have said. Be gone.
What!   [*Exeunt* LOVELL *and* DENNY.
CRAN. [*Aside*]. I am fearful—wherefore frowns he thus? | Lines 87–88 omitted.
'Tis his aspect of terror. All's not well.
KING. How now, my lord? You do desire to know
Wherefore I sent for you.
CRAN. [*Kneeling*.]   It is my duty   90
T'attend your Highness' pleasure.
KING.   Pray you, arise,
My good and gracious Lord of Canterbury.
Come, you and I must walk a turn together;
I have news to tell you; come, come, give me your hand.
Ah, my good lord, I grieve at what I speak,   95
And am right sorry to repeat what follows.

I have, and most unwillingly, of late
Heard many grievous—I do say, my lord,
Grievous—complaints of you ; which, being consider'd,
Have mov'd us and our Council that you shall   100
This morning come before us ; where I know
You cannot with such freedom purge yourself
But that, till further trial in those charges
Which will require your answer, you must take
Your patience to you and be well contented   105
To make your house our Tow'r.   You a brother of us,
It fits we thus proceed, or else no witness
Would come against you.

CRAN.   I humbly thank your Highness,
And am right glad to catch this good occasion
Most throughly to be winnowed where my chaff   110
And corn shall fly asunder ; for I know
There's none stands under more calumnious tongues
Than I myself, poor man.

KING.   Stand up, good Canterbury ;
Thy truth and thy integrity is rooted
In us, thy friend.   Give me thy hand, stand up ;   115
Prithee let's walk.   Now, by my holidame,
What manner of man are you ?   My lord, I look'd
You would have given me your petition that
I should have ta'en some pains to bring together
Yourself and your accusers, and to have heard you   120
Without indurance further.

CRAN.   Most dread liege,
The good I stand on is my truth and honesty ;
If they shall fail, I with mine enemies
Will triumph o'er my person ; which I weigh not,
Being of those virtues vacant.   I fear nothing   125
What can be said against me.

KING.   Know you not
How your state stands i' th' world, with the whole world ?
Your enemies are many, and not small ; their practices
Must bear the same proportion ; and not ever
The justice and the truth o' th' question carries   130
The due o' th' verdict with it ; at what ease
Might corrupt minds procure knaves as corrupt
To swear against you ?   Such things have been done.
You are potently oppos'd, and with a malice
Of as great size.   Ween you of better luck,   135
I mean in perjur'd witness, than your Master,
Whose minister you are, whiles here He liv'd
Upon this naughty earth ?   Go to, go to ;
You take a precipice for no leap of danger,
And woo your own destruction.

CRAN.   God and your Majesty   140
Protect mine innocence, or I fall into
The trap is laid for me !

KING.   Be of good cheer ;
They shall no more prevail than we give way to.
Keep comfort to you, and this morning see

You do appear before them ; if they shall chance,   145
In charging you with matters, to commit you,
The best persuasions to the contrary
Fail not to use, and with what vehemency
Th' occasion shall instruct you.   If entreaties
Will render you no remedy, this ring   150
Deliver them, and your appeal to us
There make before them.   Look, the good man weeps !
He's honest, on mine honour.   God's blest Mother !
I swear he is true-hearted, and a soul
None better in my kingdom.   Get you gone,   155
And do as I have bid you.   [*Exit* CRANMER.
He has strangled his language in his tears.

Enter OLD LADY.

GENT. [*Within.*]   Come back ; what mean you ?   LOVELL for GENT.
OLD L.   I'll not come back ; the tidings that I bring
Will make my boldness manners.   Now, good angels
Fly o'er thy royal head, and shade thy person   160
Under their blessed wings !
KING.   Now, by thy looks
I guess thy message.   Is the Queen deliver'd ?
Say ay, and of a boy.
OLD L.   Ay, ay, my liege ;
And of a lovely boy.   The God of Heaven
Both now and ever bless her !   'Tis a girl,   165
Promises boys hereafter.   Sir, your queen
Desires your visitation, and to be
Acquainted with this stranger ; 'tis as like you
As cherry is to cherry.
KING.   Lovell !

Enter LOVELL.

LOV.   Sir ?
KING.   Give her an hundred marks.   I'll to the Queen.   [*Exit.*
OLD L.   An hundred marks ?   By this light, I'll ha' more !
An ordinary groom is for such payment.
I will have more, or scold it out of him.
Said I for this the girl was like to him !   I'll
Have more, or else unsay't ; and now, while 'tis hot,   175
I'll put it to the issue.   [*Exeunt.*

SCENE II.   *Lobby before the Council Chamber.*   SCENE 34
                                                              Exterior. London. A
Enter CRANMER, ARCHBISHOP OF CANTERBURY.   *Courtyard in the Royal*
                                                              Palace. Day.
CRAN.   I hope I am not too late ; and yet the gentleman   CRANMER appears at
That was sent to me from the Council pray'd me   the gate.
To make great haste.   All fast ?   What means this ?   Ho!
Who waits there ?   Sure you know me ?

Enter KEEPER.

KEEP.   Yes, my lord ;
But yet I cannot help you.   5
CRAN.   Why ?

KEEP. Your Grace must wait till you be call'd for.

Enter DOCTOR BUTTS.

CRAN.   So.
BUTTS. [*Aside.*] This is a piece of malice.   I am glad
  I came this way so happily ; the King
  Shall understand it presently.   [*Exit.*
CRAN. [*Aside.*]   'Tis Butts,   10
  The King's physician ; as he pass'd along,
  How earnestly he cast his eyes upon me !
  Pray heaven he sound not my disgrace !   For certain,
  This is of purpose laid by some that hate me—
  God turn their hearts ! I never sought their malice—   15
  To quench mine honour ; they would shame to make me
  Wait else at door, a fellow councillor,
  'Mong boys, grooms, and lackeys.   But their pleasures
  Must be fulfill'd, and I attend with patience.

Enter the KING *and* BUTTS *at a window above.*

SCENE 35
*Interior. London. A
Corridor in the Royal
Palace. Day.*
The KING and BUTTS
stand by a window
looking down into the
Courtyard.

BUTTS. I'll show your Grace the strangest sight—   20
KING.   What's that, Butts ?
BUTTS. I think your Highness saw this many a day.
KING. Body a me, where is it ?
BUTTS.   There my lord :
  The high promotion of his Grace of Canterbury ;
  Who holds his state at door, 'mongst pursuivants,
  Pages, and footboys.
KING.   Ha, 'tis he indeed.   25
  Is this the honour they do one another ?
  'Tis well there's one above 'em yet. I had thought
  They had parted so much honesty among 'em—
  At least good manners—as not thus to suffer
  A man of his place, and so near our favour,   30
  To dance attendance on their lordships' pleasures,
  And at the door too, like a post with packets.
  By holy Mary, Butts, there's knavery !
  Let 'em alone, and draw the curtain close ;
  We shall hear more anon.   [*Exeunt.*

Lines 34–35 omitted.

SCENE III.   *The Council Chamber.*

*A Council table brought in, with chairs and stools, and placed under the
state.   Enter* LORD CHANCELLOR, *places himself at the upper end of
the table on the left hand, a seat being left void above him, as for
Canterbury's seat.* DUKE OF SUFFOLK, DUKE OF NORFOLK, SURREY,
LORD CHAMBERLAIN, GARDINER, *seat themselves in order on each side ;*
CROMWELL *at lower end, as secretary.* KEEPER *at the door.*

SCENE 36
*Interior. London. The
Royal Palace. The
Council Chamber. Day.*

CHAN. Speak to the business, master secretary ;
  Why are we met in council ?
CROM.   Please your honours,
  The chief cause concerns his Grace of Canterbury.
GAR. Has he had knowledge of it ?
CROM.   Yes.
NOR.   Who waits there ?

KEEP. Without, my noble lords ?
GAR.   Yes.
KEEP.   My Lord Archbishop ;   5
  And has done half an hour, to know your pleasures.
CHAN. Let him come in.
KEEP.   Your Grace may enter now.

CRANMER *approaches the Council table.*

CHAN. My good Lord Archbishop, I am very sorry
  To sit here at this present, and behold
  That chair stand empty ; but we all are men,   10
  In our own natures frail and capable
  Of our flesh ; few are angels ; out of which frailty
  And want of wisdom, you, that best should teach us,
  Have misdemean'd yourself, and not a little,
  Toward the King first, then his laws, in filling   15
  The whole realm by your teaching and your chaplains—
  For so we are inform'd—with new opinions,
  Divers and dangerous ; which are heresies,
  And, not reform'd, may prove pernicious.
GAR. Which reformation must be sudden too,   20
  My noble lords ; for those that tame wild horses
  Pace 'em not in their hands to make 'em gentle,
  But stop their mouth with stubborn bits and spur 'em
  Till they obey the manage.   If we suffer,
  Out of our easiness and childish pity   25
  To one man's honour, this contagious sickness,
  Farewell all physic ; and what follows then ?
  Commotions, uproars, with a general taint
  Of the whole state ; as of late days our neighbours,
  The upper Germany, can dearly witness,   30
  Yet freshly pitied in our memories.
CRAN. My good lords, hitherto in all the progress
  Both of my life and office, I have labour'd,
  And with no little study, that my teaching
  And the strong course of my authority   35
  Might go one way, and safely ; and the end
  Was ever to do well.   Nor is there living—
  I speak it with a single heart, my lords—
  A man that more detests, more stirs against,
  Both in his private conscience and his place,   40
  Defacers of a public peace than I do.
  Pray heaven the King may never find a heart
  With less allegiance in it !   Men that make
  Envy and crooked malice nourishment
  Dare bite the best.   I do beseech your lordships   45
  That, in this case of justice, my accusers,
  Be what they will, may stand forth face to face
  And freely urge against me.
SUF.   Nay, my lord,
  That cannot be ; you are a councillor,
  And by that virtue no man dare accuse you.   50
GAR. My lord, because we have business of more moment,

We will be short with you. 'Tis his Highness' pleasure
And our consent, for better trial of you,
From hence you be committed to the Tower;
Where, being but a private man again,   55
You shall know many dare accuse you boldly,
More than, I fear, you are provided for.
CRAN. Ah, my good Lord of Winchester, I thank you;
You are always my good friend; if your will pass,
I shall both find your lordship judge and juror,   60
You are so merciful.   I see your end—
'Tis my undoing.   Love and meekness, lord,
Become a churchman better than ambition;
Win straying souls with modesty again,
Cast none away.   That I shall clear myself,   65
Lay all the weight ye can upon my patience,
I make as little doubt as you do conscience
In doing daily wrongs.   I could say more,
But reverence to your calling makes me modest.
GAR. My lord, my lord, you are a sectary;   70
That's the plain truth.   Your painted gloss discovers,
To men that understand you, words and weakness.
CROM. My Lord of Winchester, y'are a little,
By your good favour, too sharp; men so noble,
However faulty, yet should find respect   75
For what they have been; 'tis a cruelty
To load a falling man.
GAR.   Good Master Secretary,
I cry your honour mercy; you may, worst
Of all this table, say so.
CROM.   Why, my lord?
GAR. Do not I know you for a favourer   80
Of this new sect?   Ye are not sound.
CROM.   Not sound?
GAR. Not sound, I say.
CROM.   Would you were half so honest!
Men's prayers then would seek you, not their fears.
GAR. I shall remember this bold language.
CROM.   Do.
Remember your bold life too.
CHAN.   This is too much;   85
Forbear, for shame, my lords.
GAR.   I have done.
CROM.   And I.
CHAN. Then thus for you, my lord: it stands agreed,
I take it, by all voices, that forthwith
You be convey'd to th' Tower a prisoner;
There to remain till the King's further pleasure   90
Be known unto us.   Are you all agreed, lords?
ALL. We are.
CRAN. Is there no other way of mercy,
But I must needs to th' Tower, my lords?
GAR.   What other
Would you expect?   You are strangely troublesome.
Let some o' th' guard be ready there.

Enter the Guard.

CRAN.   For me ?   95   Guard *enters now.*
  Must I go like a traitor thither ?
GAR.   Receive him,
  And see him safe i' th' Tower.
CRAN.   Stay, good my lords,
  I have a little yet to say.   Look there, my lords ;
  By virtue of that ring I take my cause
  Out of the gripes of cruel men and give it   100
  To a most noble judge, the King my master.
CHAM. This is the King's ring.
SUR.   'Tis no counterfeit.
SUF. 'Tis the right ring, by heav'n.   I told ye all,
  When we first put this dangerous stone a-rolling,
  'Twould fall upon ourselves.
NOR.   Do you think, my lords,   105
  The King will suffer but the little finger
  Of this man to be vex'd ?
CHAM.   'Tis now too certain ;
  How much more is his life in value with him !
  Would I were fairly out on't !
CROM.   My mind gave me,
  In seeking tales and informations   110
  Against this man—whose honesty the devil
  And his disciples only envy at—
  Ye blew the fire that burns ye.   Now have at ye !

Enter the KING *frowning on them ; he takes his seat.* | The KING **does not take**
                                                                    his seat.

GAR. Dread sovereign, how much are we bound to heaven
  In daily thanks, that gave us such a prince ;   115
  Not only good and wise but most religious ;
  One that in all obedience makes the church
  The chief aim of his honour and, to strengthen
  That holy duty, out of dear respect,
  His royal self in judgment comes to hear   120
  The cause betwixt her and this great offender.
KING. You were ever good at sudden commendations,   **The** KING **walks around**
  Bishop of Winchester.   But know I come not   **the Council table.**
  To hear such flattery now, and in my presence
  They are too thin and bare to hide offences.   125
  To me you cannot reach you play the spaniel,
  And think with wagging of your tongue to win me ;
  But whatsoe'er thou tak'st me for, I'm sure
  Thou hast a cruel nature and a bloody.
  [*To* CRANMER.] Good man, sit down.   Now let me see the proudest
  He that dares most but wag his finger at thee.   131
  By all that's holy, he had better starve
  Than but once think this place becomes thee not.
SUR. May it please your Grace—
KING.   No, sir, it does not please me.
  I had thought I had had men of some understanding   135
  And wisdom of my Council ; but I find none.
  Was it discretion, lords, to let this man,

This good man—few of you deserve that title—
This honest man, wait like a lousy footboy
At chamber door ? and one as great as you are ?   140
Why, what a shame was this ! Did my commission
Bid ye so far forget yourselves ? I gave ye
Power as he was a councillor to try him,
Not as a groom. There's some of ye, I see,
More out of malice than integrity,   145
Would try him to the utmost, had ye mean
Which ye shall never have while I live.

CHAN.   Thus far,
My most dread sovereign, may it like your Grace
To let my tongue excuse all. What was purpos'd
Concerning his imprisonment was rather—   150
If there be faith in men—meant for his trial
And fair purgation to the world, than malice,
I'm sure, in me.

KING. Well, well, my lords, respect him ;
Take him, and use him well, he's worthy of it.
I will say thus much for him : if a prince   155
May be beholding to a subject, I
Am for his love and service so to him.
Make me no more ado, but all embrace him ;
Be friends, for shame, my lords ! My Lord of Canterbury,   The members of the
I have a suit which you must not deny me :   160   Council shake
That is, a fair young maid that yet wants baptism :   CRANMER's hand.
You must be godfather, and answer for her.

CRAN. The greatest monarch now alive may glory
In such an honour ; how may I deserve it,
That am a poor and humble subject to you ?   165

KING. Come, come, my lord, you'd spare your spoons. You shall
have
Two noble partners with you : the old Duchess of Norfolk
And Lady Marquis Dorset. Will these please you ?
Once more, my Lord of Winchester, I charge you,   170
Embrace and love this man.

GAR.   With a true heart
And brother-love I do it.

CRAN.   And let heaven
Witness how dear I hold this confirmation.

KING. Good man, those joyful tears show thy true heart.
The common voice, I see, is verified   175
Of thee, which says thus : ' Do my Lord of Canterbury
A shrewd turn and he's your friend for ever '.
Come, lords, we trifle time away ; I long
To have this young one made a Christian.
As I have made ye one, lords, one remain ;   180
So I grow stronger, you more honour gain.   [Exeunt.

SCENE IV.   The palace yard.   This scene omitted.

Noise and tumult within. Enter Porter *and his* Man.

PORT. You'll leave your noise anon, ye rascals. Do you take the
court for Paris garden ? Ye rude slaves, leave your gaping.

[*Within* : Good master porter, I belong to th' larder.

PORT. Belong to th' gallows, and be hang'd, ye rogue ! Is this a
place to roar in ? Fetch me a dozen crab-tree staves, and strong
ones ; these are but switches to 'em. I'll scratch your heads.
You must be seeing christenings ? Do you look for ale and cakes
here, you rude rascals ?

MAN. Pray, sir, be patient ; 'tis as much impossible,   10
Unless we sweep 'em from the door with cannons,
To scatter 'em as 'tis to make 'em sleep
On May-day morning ; which will never be.
We may as well push against Paul's as stir 'em.

PORT. How got they in, and be hang'd ?   15

MAN. Alas, I know not : how gets the tide in ?
As much as one sound cudgel of four foot—
You see the poor remainder—could distribute,
I made no spare, sir.

PORT.   You did nothing, sir.

MAN. I am not Samson, nor Sir Guy, nor Colbrand,   20
To mow 'em down before me ; but if I spar'd any
That had a head to hit, either young or old,
He or she, cuckold or cuckold-maker,
Let me ne'er hope to see a chine again ;
And that I would not for a cow, God save her !   25
[*Within* : Do you hear, master porter ?

PORT. I shall be with you presently, good master puppy. Keep the
door close, sirrah.

MAN. What would you have me do ?

PORT. What should you do, but knock 'em down by th' dozens ?
Is this Moorfields to muster in ? Or have we some strange
Indian with the great tool come to court, the women so besiege
us ? Bless me, what a fry of fornication is at door ! On my
Christian conscience, this one christening will beget a thousand :
here will be father, godfather, and all together.   36

MAN. The spoons will be the bigger, sir. There is a fellow somewhat
near the door, he should be a brazier by his face, for, o' my
conscience, twenty of the dog-days now reign in's nose ; all that
stand about him are under the line, they need no other penance.
That fire-drake did I hit three times on the head, and three times
was his nose discharged against me ; he stands there like a
mortar-piece, to blow us. There was a haberdasher's wife of
small wit near him, that rail'd upon me till her pink'd porringer
fell off her head, for kindling such a combustion in the state.
I miss'd the meteor once, and hit that woman, who cried out
' Clubs ! ' when I might see from far some forty truncheoners
draw to her succour, which were the hope o' th' Strand, where
she was quartered. They fell on ; I made good my place. At
length they came to th' broomstaff to me ; I defied 'em still ;
when suddenly a file of boys behind 'em, loose shot, deliver'd
such a show'r of pebbles that I was fain to draw mine honour in
and let 'em win the work : the devil was amongst 'em, I think
surely.   56

PORT. These are the youths that thunder at a playhouse and fight for
bitten apples ; that no audience but the tribulation of Tower-hill
or the limbs of Limehouse, their dear brothers, are able to endure.

This scene omitted.

I have some of 'em in Limbo Patrum, and there they are like to
dance these three days; besides the running banquet of two
beadles that is to come.

    Enter the LORD CHAMBERLAIN.

CHAM. Mercy o' me, what a multitude are here !
 They grow still too ; from all parts they are coming,   65
 As if we kept a fair here ! Where are these porters,
 These lazy knaves ? Y'have made a fine hand, fellows.
 There's a trim rabble let in : are all these
 Your faithful friends o' th' suburbs ? We shall have
 Great store of room, no doubt, left for the ladies,   70
 When they pass back from the christening.
PORT.   An't please your honour,
 We are but men ; and what so many may do,
 Not being torn a pieces, we have done.
 An army cannot rule 'em.
CHAM.   As I live,
 If the King blame me for't, I'll lay ye all   75
 By th' heels, and suddenly ; and on your heads
 Clap round fines for neglect. Y'are lazy knaves ;
 And here ye lie baiting of bombards, when
 Ye should do service. Hark ! the trumpets sound ;
 Th'are come already from the christening.   80
 Go break among the press and find a way out
 To let the troops pass fairly, or I'll find
 A Marshalsea shall hold ye play these two months.
PORT. Make way there for the Princess.
MAN.   You great fellow,
 Stand close up, or I'll make your head ache.   85
PORT. You i' th' camlet, get up o' th' rail ;
 I'll peck you o'er the pales else.   [*Exeunt.*

    SCENE V. *The palace.*

Enter Trumpets, *sounding ; then two* ALDERMEN, LORD MAYOR, GARTER,
 CRANMER, DUKE OF NORFOLK, *with his marshal's staff,* DUKE OF
 SUFFOLK, *two* Noblemen *bearing great standing-bowls for the
 christening gifts ; then four* Noblemen *bearing a canopy, under
 which the* DUCHESS OF NORFOLK, *godmother, bearing the* CHILD
 richly habited in a mantle, &c., train borne by a LADY ; *then
 follows the* MARCHIONESS DORSET, *the other godmother, and* LADIES.
 The troop pass once about the stage, and GARTER *speaks.*

GART. Heaven, from thy endless goodness, send prosperous life, long
 and ever-happy, to the high and mighty Princess of England,
 Elizabeth !

    Flourish. Enter KING *and* GUARD.

CRAN. [*Kneeling.*] And to your royal Grace and the good Queen !
 My noble partners and myself thus pray :   5
 All comfort, joy, in this most gracious lady,
 Heaven ever laid up to make parents happy,
 May hourly fall upon ye !

This scene omitted.

SCENE 37
*Interior. London. The
Royal Palace. A Small
Chamber. Day.*
The infant Princess
Elizabeth is christened
by the Archbishop of
Canterbury.

SCENE 38
*Interior. London. The
Royal Palace. A
Chamber. Day.*
The KING enters to join
those who have
gathered to celebrate
the christening of the
young Princess.

Omitted.

KING. Thank you, good Lord Archbishop.
      What is her name ?
CRAN.   Elizabeth.
KING.   Stand up, lord.
                      [*The* KING *kisses the child.*
  With this kiss take my blessing : God protect thee !   10
  Into whose hand I give thy life.
CRAN.   Amen.
KING. My noble gossips, y'have been too prodigal ;
  I thank ye heartily.   So shall this lady,
  When she has so much English.
CRAN.   Let me speak, sir,
  For heaven now bids me ; and the words I utter   15
  Let none think flattery, for they'll find 'em truth.
  This royal infant—heaven still move about her !—
  Though in her cradle, yet now promises
  Upon this land a thousand thousand blessings,
  Which time shall bring to ripeness. She shall be—   20
  But few now living can behold that goodness—
  A pattern to all princes living with her,
  And all that shall succeed. Saba was never
  More covetous of wisdom and fair virtue
  Than this pure soul shall be. All princely graces   25
  That mould up such a mighty piece as this is,
  With all the virtues that attend the good,
  Shall still be doubled on her. Truth shall nurse her,
  Holy and heavenly thoughts still counsel her ;
  She shall be lov'd and fear'd. Her own shall bless her :   30
  Her foes shake like a field of beaten corn,
  And hang their heads with sorrow. Good grows with her;
  In her days every man shall eat in safety
  Under his own vine what he plants, and sing
  The merry songs of peace to all his neighbours.   35
  God shall be truly known ; and those about her
  From her shall read the perfect ways of honour,
  And by those claim their greatness, not by blood.
  Nor shall this peace sleep with her ; but as when
  The bird of wonder dies, the maiden phœnix,   40
  Her ashes new create another heir
  As great in admiration as herself,
  So shall she leave her blessedness to one—
  When heaven shall call her from this cloud of darkness—
  Who from the sacred ashes of her honour   45
  Shall star-like rise, as great in fame as she was,
  And so stand fix'd. Peace, plenty, love, truth, terror,
  That were the servants to this chosen infant,
  Shall then be his, and like a vine grow to him ;
  Wherever the bright sun of heaven shall shine,   50
  His honour and the greatness of his name
  Shall be, and make new nations ; he shall flourish,
  And like a mountain cedar reach his branches
  To all the plains about him ; our children's children
  Shall see this and bless heaven.
KING.   Thou speakest wonders.   55

CRAN. She shall be, to the happiness of England,
    An aged princess ; many days shall see her,
    And yet no day without a deed to crown it.
    Would I had known no more !   But she must die—
    She must, the saints must have her—yet a virgin ;   60
    A most unspotted lily shall she pass
    To th' ground, and all the world shall mourn her.
KING. O Lord Archbishop,
    Thou hast made me now a man ; never before
    This happy child did I get anything.   65
    This oracle of comfort has so pleas'd me
    That when I am in heaven I shall desire
    To see what this child does, and praise my Maker.
    I thank ye all.   To you, my good Lord Mayor,
    And you, good brethren, I am much beholding ;   70
    I have receiv'd much honour by your presence,
    And ye shall find me thankful.   Lead the way, lords.
    Ye must all see the Queen, and she must thank ye,
    She will be sick else.   This day, no man think
    Has business at his house ; for all shall stay.   75
    This little one shall make it holiday.   *Exeunt.*

THE EPILOGUE

'Tis ten to one this play can never please
All that are here.   Some come to take their ease
And sleep an act or two ; but those, we fear,
W'have frighted with our trumpets ; so, 'tis clear,
They'll say 'tis nought ; others to hear the city   5
Abus'd extremely, and to cry ' That's witty ! '
Which we have not done neither ; that, I fear,
All the expected good w'are like to hear
For this play at this time is only in
The merciful construction of good women ;   10
For such a one we show'd 'em.   If they smile
And say 'twill do, I know within a while
All the best men are ours ; for 'tis ill hap
If they hold when their ladies bid 'em clap.

The Epilogue omitted.

GLOSSARY

Scott Shane

Difficult phrases are listed under the most important or most difficult word in them. If no such word stands out, they are listed under the first word.

Words appear in the form they take in the text. If they occur in several forms, they are listed under the root form (singular for nouns, infinitive for verbs).

Line references are given only when the same word is used with different meanings, and when there are puns.

Line numbers for prose passages are counted from the last numbered line before the line referred to (since the numbers given do not always correspond to the lines in this edition).

'A, he

A GOD'S NAME, in God's name

A PIECES, to pieces

ABBEY, Westminster Abbey in London (IV i 57)

ABHOR, protest against (a legal term) (II iv 81)

ABJECT OBJECT, object of contempt

ABLE, (i) vigorous (II ii 139); (ii) sufficient (IV ii 153)

ABODED, foretold

ABOUND, prosper

ABROAD, (i) out of one's house or room (I iv 5, III ii 83); (ii) current, talked about (III ii 391)

ACQUAINTED, informed

ACTION'S, 'Which action's self was tongue to', which was displayed in the actual events

ADMIRATION, ability to arouse wonder

ADMIT, allow

ADVERTISE, inform

ADVIS'D, 'Be advis'd', take care

AFFECT, aspire to (II iii 29) ; 'affect In honour honesty', love truth as an honourable man should

AFFLICTED, troubled

AGAINST, (i) in preparation for (III i 25); (ii) toward (III ii 118)

AGUE, fever

AIR'D THEM, exposed them to the air (with pun on 'heired them', made them heirs)

ALE AND CAKES, traditionally served at celebrations

ALLAY, moderate, restrain

ALLEGED, stated, put forward

ALLEGIANT, loyal

ALLOWANCE, permission

ALLOW'D, approved, acknowledged

AN, if; 'an't', if it; 'An if', if indeed

ANON, soon

ANSWER, 'to his answer', to answer the charges against him

APPLIANCE ONLY, only remedy

APPOINTMENT, orders

APPROVE THE FAIR CONCEIT, confirm the good opinion

APT TO ACCUSE, predisposed to find fault with

ARCH, chief, pre-eminent

ARGUE, discuss

ART, learning

ARTICLES, (i) terms (of a treaty) (I i 169); (ii) items in an indictment (III ii 293, 299, 304)

ASPECT, look, expression

ASSISTANTS, both (i) ministers of state; and (ii) supporters, associates

ASUNDER, apart

AT ONCE, all at once

ATTACH, (i) seize by order of law (I i 95); (ii) arrest (I i 217, I ii 210)

ATTAINDER, disgrace and dismissal

ATTEND, wait, await

AUGHT, anything

AUTHORS, originators, perpetrators

AVAUNT, dismissal, order to leave

AVOID, leave

AXE WITH THE EDGE TOWARDS HIM, traditionally a sign of impending execution

AY, yes

BAITING OF BOMBARDS, drinking from leathern jugs

BAYS, bay leaves (symbolic of joy and triumph)

BEADLES, officers of the law

BEHOLDING, indebted

BELONG, 'belong to worship', hold noble rank; 'No great offence belongs to 't', no serious breach of propriety in revealing it; 'belong to th' larder', am employed in the pantry

BENEFITS, natural gifts

BESEECH, ask, I ask

BESHREW ME, evil befall me (a mild oath)

BETWIXT, between

BEVIS, Saxon knight, celebrated in ballads and romances for feats of arms

BEVY, company of ladies

BEWAILING, mourning

BIG LOOK, arrogant expression

BLACK MOUTH, evil tongue

BLACKFRIARS, Dominican monastery in London

BLIND PRIEST, i.e. Wolsey has inherited the arbitrariness and inconstancy of Fortune (often depicted as blind and turning a wheel)

BLIST'RED, puffed

BLOW US, blow us up

BLUSHING, glowing (III ii 354)

BODY A ME, body of me (a mild oath)

BOOK, book-learning

BOOTLESS, profitless

BORES, cheats

BOSOM UP, keep secret

BOUND, indebted

BOW'D, 'threepence bow'd', bent (and thus worthless) coin (with pun on 'threepence bawd')

BRAKE, thicket

BRASS, 'live in brass', are remembered forever

BRAZIER, brass-worker

BREACH OF DUTY, violation of decorum

BREAK, check (III ii 198); 'breaks The sides', bursts the bounds; 'broken with', disclosed to; 'break among', force a path through

BREATH, 'with a breath', in the space of one breath

BREEDING, 'virtuous breeding', good up-bringing

BRING ME OFF, save me

BROACH THIS BUSINESS, raise this subject

BROILING, suffering great heat

BROKEN, interrupted (I iv 61)

BROOMSTAFF, 'to th' broomstaff to me', a club's length from me

BROTHER, 'You a brother of us', you being a member of our council

BUTCHER'S CUR, Wolsey, who was thought to have been the son of a butcher

BUZZING, rumour

CALUMNIOUS, slanderous

CAMLET, fine cloth

CAPABLE OF, subject to the weaknesses of

CARDERS, workers who comb impurities out of the wool

CARDINAL, 'cardinal virtues', the four essential virtues of fortitude, justice, prudence, and temperance; 'cardinal sins', the seven deadly sins (with puns on Wolsey's and Campeius' office)

CARNARVONSHIRE, a poor and barren Welsh county

CARRIAGE, behaviour

CARRY, (i) manage (I i 100, I ii 134); (ii) behave (II iv 143)

CAUTION, warning

CENSURE, (i) judgement (I i 33); (ii) rebuke (III i 64)

CERTAIN, certainly

CERTES, certainly

CHAFED, angry

CHALKS, 'whose grace Chalks successors their way', whose virtue marks out a path to advancement for those who follow

CHALLENGE, objection (a legal term for the rejection of a juryman)

CHAMBERS DISCHARG'D, small cannons fired

CHANCE TO, happen to

CHANCELLOR, secretary

CHANGES, movements in the dance

CHARTREUX, Carthusian monastic order

CHATTELS, movable goods

CHERUBINS, cherubs (childlike angelic creatures), or their ornate sculptural representations

CHEVERIL, flexible, elastic (like 'cheveril', or kid-leather)

CHIDING, tumultuous and noisy

CHINE, joint of beef

CHOICE HOUR, convenient time

CHOLER, anger

CINQUE-PORTS, the barons of the Channel ports of Dover, Hastings, Hythe, Romney, and Sandwich

CITED, summoned

CLAPP'D, fastened

CLERKS, scholars

CLINQUANT, glittering

CLOSE, (i) aside, out of sight (II i 55, IV i 36);

(ii) shut (V ii 34, V iv 28)

CLOTH, 'cloth of state', canopy above the throne; 'cloth of honour', canopy

CLOUD OF DARKNESS, i.e. earth

CLUBS, cry rallying London apprentices to a fight

COASTS AND HEDGES, moves indirectly and secretly toward

COAT, 'long coat', i.e. clergyman's robes

COLBRAND, legendary Danish giant

COLD, coldness (a sign of death) (IV ii 98)

COLLARS OF ESSES, gold chains formed of S-shaped links

COLLECTED OUT OF, gathered concerning

COLOUR, pretext

COLT'S TOOTH IS NOT CAST, youthful wildness is not cast off

COMBINATION, treaty

COMMEND, (i) entrust (IV ii 131, V i 17); (ii) 'Commends his good opinion of you', sends his compliments (II iii 61)

COMMENDATIONS, (i) greetings (IV ii 118); (ii) compliments (V iii 122)

COMMISSION, legal mandate, warrant (for the collection of taxes and other purposes)

COMMIT, (i) send to prison (I ii 193, V i 146, V iii 54); (ii) 'committed . . . to doubt', refrained from offering (II iv 214–15)

COMMONALTY, common people

COMMONS, the common people and their representatives in Parliament

COMPASS, 'Beyond thought's compass', exceeding wildest imagination

COMPELL'D FORTUNE, fortune which is forced upon you

COMPLETE, perfect

COMPTROLLERS, stewards in charge of household expenditure; here, probably equivalent to 'masters of ceremonies'

CONCEIT, 'fair conceit', good opinion

CONCEPTION, design

CONCLAVE, 'holy conclave', College of Cardinals

CONDITION, 'true condition', loyal character

CONDUCT, 'under your fair conduct', by your kind allowance

CONFEDERACY, conspiracy

CONFERENCE, conversation

CONFIDENT, 'I am confident', I trust you

CONFORMABLE, obedient

CONGEE, bow reverently

CONJUNCTION, marriage

CONSEQUENCE OF DREAD, fearful consequences

CONSISTORY, ecclesiastical court; 'Consistory of Rome', College of Cardinals

CONSTANCY, persistence

CONSTANT WOMAN TO, woman faithful to

CONSTRUCTION, interpretation

CONSULTING, 'not consulting', independently, without consulting the others

CONTRARY (n.), opposing side; 'i' th' contrary', in the opposite case

CONTRARY PROCEEDINGS, actions contradicting their outward appearances

CONVENTED, summoned

COPE, encounter

CORN, wheat

CORNER, 'a corner', i.e. secrecy

COUNT, i.e. one rank lower than a duke (with sexual pun)

COUNT-CARDINAL, i.e. cardinal of humble birth behaving like a count

COURSES OF THE SUN, years

COVENT, convent (applied to religious companies of either sex)

COW, 'not for a cow', i.e. not for anything

CRAB-TREE STAVES, cudgels made of crab-apple (a very hard wood)

CRAVE, ask

CREATURE, dependent (III ii 36)

CREDIT, (i) belief (I i 37); (ii) good reputation (III ii 265)

CROSS (adj.), perverse; (v.), oppose

CROWN (n.), 'high feats done to th' crown', great services done for the king; (v.), confirm (by giving you offices) (III ii 155)

CRY, declare (I i 27); 'cry down', put down, overcome; 'cried up', praised; 'Cry thee amen', agree with what you say; 'cry your honour mercy', beg your pardon

CUM PRIVILEGIO, by special licence; i.e. with immunity

CURE (n.), (i) group of parishioners; (ii) remedy (for frowning) (pun, I iv 33); (v.), remedy

DAM, mother

DANCE ATTENDANCE ON, wait submissively on

DANGER SERVES AMONG THEM, they welcome danger as a comrade

DARE, 'Daring th' event to th' teeth', daring the worst in open defiance; 'dare us with his cap', dazzle us with his scarlet cap (as hunters dazzled larks with a mirror or a piece of red cloth); 'dare your worst objections', defy your most serious accusations

DASHING THE GARMENT, violently striking the substance

DEAR RESPECT, heartfelt regard

DEATH, by God's death (an oath) (I iii 13)

DECEIV'D, disappointed

DECLINE, fall from prosperity

DEEM, think

DEEP ENVIOUS, deeply malicious

DEFACERS, destroyers

DEFEAT THE LAW, refute the charges

DELIVER, relate

DEMI-CORONAL, small crown

DEMURE, solemn

DERIV'D, drawn

DESIRE, request

DETERMINATE RESOLUTION, final settlement

DEVICE, (i) trickery (I i 204); (ii) scheme (III ii 217)

DIFFERENCE, (i) dispute (I i 101, III i 58); (ii) distinction of rank (I i 139)

DIGEST, stomach, put up with

DIGNITIES, high position, title

DISCERNER, spectator

DISCOURSER, storyteller

DISCOVERS, reveals

DISPLEASURE, disgrace (III ii 392)

DISPOSE, (i) direct (I ii 116); (ii) 'To the disposing of it nought rebelled', there was not a single jarring element in the arrangement of the pageantry

DISTRACTION, 'mere distraction', sheer madness

DIVERS, various

DIVORCE OF STEEL, axe dividing soul from body

DOG-DAYS, hottest days of the year (about 3 July to 15 August, when Sirius, the Dog-Star, rises with the sun)

DOING, actions

DOMESTICS, servants

DOUBLE, deceitfully ambiguous

DOUBLETS, men's close-fitting jackets

DOUBTED, suspected

DOWAGER, titled widow

DUE O' TH' VERDICT, just verdict

DULL, inanimate and gloomy

DULY HALLOWED, sufficiently holy

DURST, dare, dared

DWELL IN, continue

EAGERLY, sharply

EASE, 'at what ease', how easily

EASINESS, indulgence

EASY, gullible, easily persuaded (III ii 356)

EFFECTS, appearances

EGO ET REX MEUS, my king and I (though this is the normal Latin word order, Shakespeare followed his sources in having the placing of *Ego*, 'I', imply an insult to the king)

ELEMENT, 'promises no element', would not be expected to take part

EMBALLING, investment with the ball which symbolises royalty (with sexual suggestion)

END, object, purpose; 'The Cardinal is the end', the Cardinal is at the root

ENVIOUS, malicious

ENVY (n.), malice, hatred

ENVY AT, hate

EQUAL, (i) just as (I i 159); (ii) fair, just (II ii 105, II iv 18)

ERE, before

ESTATE, (i) state (II ii 67, IV i 36 stage direction); (ii) condition (V i 74)

EVEN, (i) just (III i 37); (ii) tranquil (III i 166)

EVER, always

EVIL US'D, badly treated

EVILS, possibly 'privies'; more likely, 'evil structures'

EXACTION, tax

EXAMINATION, paper containing the testimony of a witness

EXAMPLE, precedent

EXCEEDING, exceedingly

EXCLAMATION, reproach

EXHALATION, meteor

EXTREMELY, profusely (II i 33)

EXTREMITY, 'in great extremity', in grave danger

FACULTIES, personal qualities

FAIL, 'our fail', both (i) my failure to beget an heir; and (ii) my death; 'issue's fail', failure to beget an heir

FAIN, (i) gladly (II i 24); (ii) obliged (V iv 52)

FAINTS ME, makes me faint

FAIRLY, properly

FAITH, (i) indeed (I i 167, I iii 16, I iv 17); (ii) trustworthiness, loyalty (II i 143, 145, III i 53, V iii 151)

FALL, comes to pass (II i 141); 'fell to himself', came to himself; 'fell off', moved back; 'fell on', attacked

FALLING ONES, (i) meteors; (ii) women who fall from virtue (pun, IV i 55)

FAME, report

FANCY, imagination, thoughts; 'particular fancy', private imaginings

FAR, extreme (III i 65)

FASHION, nature, shape

FAST, shut

FATHER, father-in-law (II i 44)

FATHOM, 'ten fathom deep', sixty feet deep; i.e. dead

FAULT, offence; 'make faults', commit offences; 'fault thou gav'st him', offence you falsely accused him of

FAVOUR, good will; 'best in favour', best-looking and most popular; 'Pray, give me favour', please hear me out

FEAR, doubt (III ii 16)

FEARFUL, afraid

FEE, pay

FELL (adj.), terrible

FELLOW, (i) term of address, used insultingly (because generally applied only to gross inferiors) (I i 151, III ii 279, IV ii 100, 107); (ii) equal (I iii 41)

FELT HIMSELF, truly knew himself

FIERCE, extravagant

FIGHTS AND FIREWORKS, duels, and both (i) fireworks; and (ii) visits to prostitutes (pun, I iii 27)

FIGURE, 'Whose figure even this instant cloud puts on', whose figure is clothed in clouds at this very moment

FIL'D, kept pace

FILE (n.), (i) list (I i 75); (ii) group (of people) (I ii 42, V iv 51)

FIRE-DRAKE, meteor (i.e. the 'brazier')

FIREWORKS, (i) fireworks; (ii) visits to prostitutes (pun, I iii 27)

FIT (n.), 'fit or two o' th' face', a grimace or two; 'last fit', last gasp; (v.), is appropriate

FITNESS, ''tis a needful fitness', it is necessary and appropriate

FLAW'D, broken

FLOURISH, fanfare

FLOWING, abundant

FOLLOWING, successive

FOOL AND FEATHER, foolish fashions in dress and conduct

FOOTBOY, youth employed as a servant

FOOTING, foot

FORCE (n.), validity (I ii 101); (v.), press (III ii 2)

FOREIGN MAN STILL, always abroad

FORESKIRT, 'honour's train Is longer than his foreskirt', more honour is to come than has yet been shown

FORFEITING OUR OWN BRAINS, giving up any claims to intelligence

FORG'D HIM, caused him to devise

FORGO, forsake

FORMER FABULOUS STORY, stories formerly considered incredible

FORSAKE, departs (from my body, at death) (II i 89)

FORSOOTH, indeed

FORTUNES, 'both my fortunes', my good and my bad fortunes

FORTY PENCE, NO, i.e. I'll bet it's not

FORWARD, eager to do

FOULNESS IS THE PUNISHMENT, the moral impurity of being disloyal is the punishment for disloyalty

FOUNTS IN JULY, streams that have cleared after spring flooding

FRAME THINGS THAT ARE KNOWN ALIKE, devise the measures which (as you claim) all know about

FRANKLY, freely

FREE, (i) freely (II ii 82); (ii) innocent (III i 32); (iii) frank (III i 60); 'free of your report', innocent of your accusations

FRESH, (i) untiring, strong (I i 3); (ii) 'fresh about me', still in my mind

FRESH-FISH, newcomer, novice

FRET THE STRING, THE MASTER-CORD, wear through the tendon, the chief sinew (with pun on 'fret' of a stringed instrument, III ii 105–6)

FRIENDED BY HIS WISH, granted his wish (that the king should die without an heir)

FRONT BUT IN THAT FILE WHERE OTHERS TELL STEPS WITH ME, merely march in the front rank along with others who keep step with me

FRUIT SHE GOES WITH, child she is bearing

FRUITFUL, generous

FRY OF FORNICATION, (i) swarm of fornicators; (ii) swarm produced by fornication

FULL, 'full hot', high-spirited; 'at full', fully

FULL-CHARG'D, fully loaded

FULLERS, workers who cleaned the wool by beating it

FURNISH, (i) supply with learning (I ii 113); (ii) equip (II ii 3, 138); (iii) supply with money (III ii 328)

FURNITURE, furnishings

FURTHER DAY, a future day

GAINSAY MY DEED, deny what I have done

GALL (n.), personal spite; (v.), 'gall'd', wounded

GAMESTER, (i) playful person; (ii) lewd person (pun, I iv 45)

GAP AND TRADE, entrance and beaten path; i.e., likelihood of receiving

GAPING, shouting

GARTER, the Garter King-at-Arms, who announced the accession of a new sovereign

GENERALLY, by everyone

GET, (i) conceive (II iii 44); (ii) achieve; (iii) beget (pun on (ii) and (iii), V v 65)

GETTING, 'unsatisfied in getting', insatiably acquisitive

GIVE, 'gav'st him', falsely accused him of; 'give way to', allow; 'My mind gave me', I had a feeling

GLADDED IN'T, made glad in this matter

GLEANING, gathering

GLIST'RING, glittering

GLOSS, 'painted gloss discovers', deceitful appearance and speech reveals

GO, 'Go to', an expression of impatience or disapproval; 'gone beyond', overreached

GOING OUT, expedition

GOOD TIME, i.e. a safe delivery

GOODLIEST, most attractive

GOSSIPS, godparents

GOVERNMENT, self-control

GRACE, (i) mercy (I ii 104); (ii) virtue (I ii 122, III ii 138, V v 25); (iii) honour (I iv 73); (iv) generosity (II iii 65, III ii 166, 174, V i 48); 'whose grace Chalks successors their way', whose virtue marks out a path to advancement for those who follow

GRIEF, grievance (I ii 56)

GRIEVANCE, distress

GRIP'D, grasped by the hand (as a sign of equality)

GRIPES, clutches

GROUNDED, 'How grounded he', on what did he base

GROW FROM THE KING'S ACQUAIN-TANCE, become estranged from the king

GRUBB'D UP, dug up by the roots

GUARDED, trimmed

GUY, 'Sir Guy', celebrated in romances for slaying the Danish giant Colbrand

GUYNES AND ARDE, two towns in Picardy, northern France

HA, Henry VIII's habitual exclamation

HABIT (n.), attire; 'habit of doctors', furred black gown and flat cap worn by Doctors of Law

HABITED (v.), dressed

HAIR, 'in her hair', with her hair hanging loosely (a bridal custom)

HALBERDS, officers carrying halberds, long-handled weapons

HALL, Westminster Hall in London

HAND, 'under your hands and seals', with your signed and sealed approval; 'her two hands', Queen Anne's two supporters; 'hand and tongue', agent and spokesman; 'a fine hand', a fine job of it (ironical)

HANGS ON, depends on

HAP, 'ill hap', bad luck

HAPPIEST, 'first and happiest hearers', finest and most favourably disposed theatre audience

HAPPILY, (i) appropriately (or, possibly, 'perhaps') (IV ii 10); (ii) opportunely (V i 85, V ii 9)

HARDLY CONCEIVE, either (i) think harshly; or (ii) have almost no conception

HARD-RUL'D, difficult to manage

HARMONY, 'celestial harmony', the music of the heavenly spheres, thought to be audible to the soul when freed from the body

HAUTBOYS, oboes

HAVE-AT-HIM, attack, challenge

HAVE AT YOU (YE), look out, here begins the attack

HAVING, possession

HE, man (V iii 131)

HEAD, 'rais'd head', gathered troops

HEALTH, toast

HEART, 'best heart', very essence

HEAVY, oppressive

HEED, (i) care (I ii 173, 175, III i 110); (ii) attention (II iv 169); (iii) serious concern (III ii 80)

HEIGHT, 'to th' height', in the highest degree

HENTON, Nicholas Hopkins (of I i 221); Henton was the name of his monastery

HERALD, (i) official who announced challenges at a tournament (I i 34); (ii) eulogist (IV ii 69)

HIGH-BLOWN, over-inflated

HITTING A GROSSER QUALITY, appealing to a lower class of people

HOLD, 'hold 'em', maintain their grimaces; 'Held current music', have it accepted as good music; 'it held not', it did not last; 'held for certain', it is thought certain; 'holds his state', maintains his dignity; 'hold ye play', keep you busy; 'If they hold', if they hold back their applause

HOLIDAME, 'by my holidame', by our Lady

HONEST, honourable (III i 154)

HONESTY, chastity (IV ii 145)

HONOUR OF IT DOES PAY THE ACT OF IT, the honour of being loyal is the reward of loyalty

HONOURABLE POINTS OF IGNORANCE, points of what the ignorant consider honourable behaviour

HOODS, 'all hoods make not monks', proverbial warning against judging by appearances

HULLING, drifting with sails furled

HUSBAND, 'ill husband', bad manager

ILL, offensive, bad; 'ill doctrine', false theology; 'Of his own body he was ill', his sexual conduct was immoral

ILLUSIONS, deceptions

IMPORTING, signifying

IN, concerning (II iv 103)

INCENSE, (i) enrage (I ii 65, III ii 61); (ii) stir up (V i 43)

INDIA, probably not India but the New World (proverbial as a source of fabulous wealth)

INDIAN, American Indian (who were frequently displayed at court as curiosities)

INDIES, 'all the Indies', i.e. great riches

INDIFFERENT, impartial

INDUCED BY POTENT CIRCUMSTANCES, persuaded by powerful evidence

INDURANCE FURTHER, further hardship

INNUMERABLE SUBSTANCE, immeasurable wealth

INTELLIGENCE, information received

INTERVIEW, ceremonial meeting

IPSWICH, Wolsey's birthplace

IPSWICH AND OXFORD, the locations of colleges founded by Wolsey

IRRESOLUTE, i.e. unaccomplished

ISSUE, (i) outcome, result (I i 87, I ii 90); (ii) offspring (I ii 134, II iv 191, 198, III ii 291); 'issue's fail', failure to beget an heir; 'put it to the issue', force a decision, try my luck

JADED, intimidated and humiliated

JEWEL, expensive gold chain worn by gentlemen

JUDGMENT, sentence (II i 32, 58)

JUGGLE, trick

JUSTIFY, confirm

KEECH, lump of fat (Wolsey was thought to have been the son of a butcher)

KEEP, 'keep state', affect grandeur; 'keep your way', keep going; 'Keep comfort to you', take comfort

KIND, expression (II iii 66); 'In what kind . . .

Is this exaction?', what form does this taxation take?

KNOCK IT, strike up

KNOW, (i) recognise (I iv 80); (ii) find out, come to understand (II ii 19, 20, 52)

LAG END, remaining part

LATE, (i) recent; (ii) former (III ii 94, IV i 33)

LAY (v.), resided (IV i 28); 'then lay by', then rested; 'of purpose laid', deliberately prepared as a trap; 'lay . . . By th' heels', put into fetters; (adj.), unreligious, secular

LEAVE (n.), permission; (v.), stop (III i 2, IV ii 94, V iv 1–2)

LEGATE, representative of the Pope in England

LEGATINE, as the Pope's representative

LEGS, 'new legs', new ways of walking and bowing

LEISURE, 'spiritual leisure', religious occupations

LEND, give

LETTERS-PATENTS, 'Tied it by letters-patents', confirmed it by a public authorisation

LEVEL, line of fire

LEWDNESS, wickedness

LIBERAL, generous

LIE I' TH' BOSOM OF, (i) marry; (ii) share the secrets of (pun, III ii 100)

LIEGE, lord

LIGHTED, dismounted

LIGHTEN, give light to (gems were believed to emit light)

LIKE (adj.), 'much like', very likely; 'was like to', resembled; 'like to dance', likely to dance; 'like to hear', likely to hear; (v.), please; 'Like it your grace', if it please your grace

LIMBO PATRUM, region in the underworld inhabited by the souls of the righteous who died before Christ's coming; here, 'prison'

LIMBS OF LIMEHOUSE, i.e. scoundrels of a rough dockyard district in London

LINE, 'under the line', on the equator

LIST, chooses

LITTLE, 'in a little', briefly

LITTLE ENGLAND, (i) England; (ii) Pembrokeshire (of which Anne is to become Marchioness)

LO, look

LOAD, oppress (V iii 77)

LOADEN, loaded

LOFTY, haughty

LONG'D, belonged

LONGER YOU DESIRE, you desire to protract the business of

'LONGING, 'The many to them 'longing', the many people employed by them

LOOK, (i) see that (II i 66); (ii) expect (V i 117)

LOOSE, (i) careless (II i 127); (ii) 'loose shot', marksmen not attached to a company (V iv 51)

LOP, smaller branches and twigs

LOSE, (i) forget (II i 57); (ii) give up (IV ii 102)

LOUSY, lice-infested

LOUVRE, the palace of the French kings in Paris

LUCIFER, rebel archangel who fell from heaven because of his pride

LUMP, lump of clay

MACE, royal sceptre, emblematic of the monarchy

MADAMS, ladies of rank

MAIDEN FLOWERS, flowers appropriate to one who lived chastely

MAIDENHEAD, virginity

MAIN, 'main power', superior force; 'main secret', all-important secret; 'main assent', general agreement

MAKE, 'makes his way', wins his advancement; 'makes a supper . . . To', gives a supper for; 'make my play', win my game (with sexual suggestion); 'hither make', are on their way here; 'make use now', take advantage of this opportunity; 'make as little doubt', have as little doubt; 'made no spare', did not spare

MAKINGS, ceremonial objects and emblems

MANAGE, commands of the horse-trainer

MANORS, 'broke their backs with laying manors on 'em', ruined themselves by pawning their estates in order to dress lavishly

MARK, pay attention to, take note of

MARKS, 'an hundred marks', almost £67 (a substantial amount)

MARRY, indeed

MARSHALSEA, prison in Southwark, London

MASKERS, costumed and masked participants in a court masque

MASQUE, courtly dramatic spectacle

MASTER, (i) teacher (I i 17); (ii) 'Master O' th' Rolls', keeper of public records (V i 34–5); (iii) Christ (V i 136)

MATE, match

MAY-DAY MORNING, 1 May (a holiday on which celebrations began before dawn)

MAZ'D CONSIDERINGS, perplexed thoughts

MEAN, means (V iii 146)

MEASURE, stately dance

MEET, take advantage of (III ii 7)

MEMORIZ'D, made memorable

MERE, sheer; 'mere distraction', sheer madness; 'mere undoing', utter ruin

MERIDIAN, the highest point of a star

METEOR, i.e. the red-faced 'brazier'

METHINKS, it seems to me

MINCING, 'Saving your mincing', with all due respect to your affectation

MINDED, 'how you stand minded in', what is your opinion of

MINISTER (n.), (i) means, agent (I i 108); (ii) servant (V i 137); (v.), 'minister communication of a most poor issue', serve to disclose a very poor result

MIRROR, model

MISCARRIED, went astray

MISCHIEF, misfortune (II i 66)

MISDEMEAN'D YOURSELF, behaved badly

MISTAKES, misjudges

MODEL, image

MODEST, temperate (V iii 69)

MODESTY, (i) gentleness (II ii 134); (ii) moderation (IV ii 74, V iii 64)

MOE, more

MOIETY, half

MOMENT, importance

MONSIEURS, i.e. English courtiers who imitate French fashions

MONUMENT, tomb

MOON, 'below the moon', i.e. worldly

MOORFIELDS, park outside London

MORROW, morning

MORTAL, 'wear our mortal state to come', spend the rest of my mortal existence

MORTAR-PIECE, a short cannon with a large bore

MOTION, (i) motive (I i 153); (ii) act (I ii 86); (iii) request (II iv 233)

MOTLEY, multi-coloured cloth traditionally worn by the professional fool

MOULD UP SUCH A MIGHTY PIECE, go to make up such a great person

MOUNT, raise

MOVE, (i) persuade, induce (II iv 167, V i 100); (ii) appeal to (II iv 209, 217); (iii) anger (V i 46); 'heaven still move about her', may God be always near her

MUD IN EGYPT, i.e. the source of its fertility and wealth

MURMURERS, grumblers

MUSIC, 'Held current music', have it accepted as good music; 'choicest music', finest musicians; 'Bid the music leave', ask the musicians to stop playing

MYSTERIES, 'such strange mysteries', such outlandish fashions

NAKED, defenceless

NAUGHTY, wicked

NEAR, closely affecting

NEW-TRIMM'D, newly fitted out for a voyage (and thus unlikely to yield any victims to the 'rav'nous fishes')

NEXT, near

NOIS'D, rumoured

NONE EFFECT, 'made of none effect', annulled

NOTE, (i) knowledge (I ii 48); (ii) melody (IV ii 78); ''a gives us note', he lets us know

NOTHING, (i) not at all (I i 207, V i 125); (ii) 'makes him nothing', annihilates him (III ii 208)

NOTWITHSTANDING THAT YOUR BOND OF DUTY, over and above your ordinary duty of loyalty

NOUGHT, (i) nothing (I i 43, II iv 135); (ii) worthless (Epilogue 5)

NUMBER, 'a number more', quite a few others; 'above a number', more than many

OBEYING IN COMMANDING, modest and self-effacing in giving commands

OBJECTIONS, accusations

O'ERMOUNT, both (i) fly higher than; and (ii) sing louder than

O'ERTOPPING, surpassing

OFFER OF THIS TIME, opportunity now offered

OFFERS (v.), shows her intention (II iv 121 SD)

OFFICE, duty, function; 'office did Distinctly his full function', each official carried out all his tasks without confusion

OFFICIOUS, interfering

OMIT THE OFFER OF THIS TIME, neglect this opportunity

ON, of (I i 94, II iii 102, II iv 151, III i 21, III ii 106, V iii 109)

ONCE WEAK ONES, in a word, weak-minded ones

ONE, 'one the wisest', the very wisest; 'one the least', the very least

ONLY BITTER TO HIM, ONLY DYING, the only bitter thing, the only thing that gives death significance

OPEN, public

OPINION, (i) reputation (Prologue 20); (ii) gossip (III i 36); 'in his opinions', i.e. not in person, but in the form of the opinions he has sent back ahead of him

OPPOSING, exposing

OPPRESSION, distress

OR . . .OR, either . . . or

ORACLE, (i) trusted counselor (III ii 104); (ii) 'oracle of comfort', comforting prophecy (V v 66)

ORDER GAVE EACH THING VIEW, everything was arranged so that it could be viewed easily

ORD'RED, arranged

ORPHEUS, musician in Greek mythology whose lyre could tame animals and control inanimate nature

OTHERWHERE, elsewhere

OUT, 'The honourable board of council out', without consulting the council; 'out of himself', beyond his own mind (I ii 114), besides himself (III ii 13); 'speak thee out', fully describe you; 'Out upon ye', shame on you (an indignant reproach)

OUTGO, surpass, exceed

OUTSPEAKS POSSESSION OF A SUBJECT, describes more than what a subject should possess

OUTWORTHS, is more highly valued than

OWN, 'Her own', her own people

PACE, walk; 'Pace 'em not in their hands', do not lead them through their paces by hand

PACK, go, clear off

PACKET, parcel of state papers

PAGE, boy or young man serving in a nobleman's retinue or at court

PAINTING, 'Was to them as a painting', coloured their faces as if with cosmetics

PANG, pain

PANGING, painful

PAPER (n.), wrapper (III ii 78)

PAPERS (v.), 'must fetch him in he papers', must obtain the services of those whom he puts on his list

PARAGON'D O' TH' WORLD, held up as a model of perfection before the world

PARCELS, items

PARIS GARDEN, popular and noisy bull- and bear-baiting arena in London

PART (n.), quality (II iii 27, II iv 139, III ii

258); 'The sixth part', one sixth; 'part of a housewife', in part a housewife; 'blessed part', soul; (v.), (i) depart (III i 97, III ii 205, IV i 92); (ii) 'parted so much honesty', shared so much decency

PARTICULAR, 'particular fancy', private imaginings; 'particular consent', specific approval; 'in love's particular', with the special consideration of love

PARTNERS, fellow-godparents

PASS, (i) be approved by (I ii 70); (ii) 'pass away', depart (I iv 33); (iii) proceed (II i 10); (iv) prevail (V iii 59)

PASSAGES MADE, steps taken

PAT, 'Come pat betwixt too early and too late', come at the right time

PAUL'S, St Paul's Cathedral in London

PAUSINGLY, hesitantly

PECK YOU O'ER THE PALES, pitch you over the railings

PEER, nobleman

PEPIN OR CLOTHARIUS, early Frankish kings

PERFIDIOUS, treacherous

PERFORCE, of necessity

PERIOD, goal

PERK'D UP, dressed up, decked out

PERNICIOUS, disastrous

PERNICIOUSLY, to death, mortally

PERSUADING, persuasive

PESTILENT, offensive

PHOENIX, legendary bird which lives without a mate for 660 years, consumes itself in flames, and rises again from its own ashes

PHRASE, describe

PHYSIC, medicine, medical treatment

PILLARS, 'two great silver pillars', Wolsey's distinctive insignia

PINCHES, torments

PITCH, level, degree of honour or dishonour

PITIED, 'Was either pitied in him or forgotten', either aroused useless pity for him, or had no effect at all

PITIFUL, compassionate

PLACE (n.), high office, position of authority; 'less place', lower rank; 'made good my place', defended my position

PLACE YOU, assign places to the guests

PLAGUE OF YOUR POLICY, a curse on your scheming

PLAINSONG, simple melody

PLATE, table service of gold and silver

PLAY, i.e. sexual play (I iii 45)

PLEASANT, merry

PLEASURE, wish, desire; 'speak your pleasures', say what you think

PLUCK OFF, come down in rank

POLICY, scheming

PORRINGER, 'pink'd porringer', ornamented round cap resembling a porridge dish

PORTION, possession

POSSESS'D HIM WITH A SCRUPLE, put a doubt in his mind

POST WITH PACKETS, courier with letters

POSTED, 'is posted', has hastened

POTENCY, power

POW'RS, powerful men

PRACTICE, evil plot, intrigue

PRÆMUNIRE, statute limiting papal jurisdiction in England

PREFERR'D FROM, promoted from being

PREJUDICE, disadvantage, detriment

PREMISES, 'upon the premises', given the evidence

PRESENCE, presence-chamber where the king or queen received visitors (III i 17, IV ii 37)

PRESENT, immediate; 'at this present', now

PRESENTLY, at once

PRESS, crowd

PRETENCE, pretext

PRIDE, lavish adornment (I i 25)

PRIME, principal

PRIMER, more urgent

PRIMERO, a fashionable card game

PRIMEST, most excellent

PRITHEE, I pray thee, please

PRIVATE, alone (II ii 12)

PRIVILEG'D, entitled to immunity

PRIVILY, secretly

PRIVITY, confidential participation

PRIVY CHAMBER, private room

PROCESS, course of events

PRODIGAL, generous with gifts

PROFESS, declare; 'Those we profess', what we claim to be

PROFESSORS, those who profess Christian faith

PRONOUNCE, declare

PROOF, (i) 'He shall appear in proof', experience will reveal him (I i 197); (ii) statement of evidence (II i 16)

PROPER TITLE OF, fine thing to call (ironical)

PROPORTION, 'bear the same proportion', be as great in number and size

PUBLISH'D, publicly proclaimed

PURGATION, vindication

PURGE, 'with such freedom purge yourself', clear yourself of guilt so easily
PURSE, bag containing the great seal, emblem of the Lord Chancellor's office
PURSUIVANTS, junior officers
PUT, 'put off', dismissed from employment; 'put me off', discard me
PUTTER-ON, instigator

QUARREL, quarreller
QUEEN IT, become queen (with pun on 'quean it', play the whore)
QUESTION (n.), (i) doubt (II iv 151); (ii) cause (V i 130); (v.), dispute
QUIET, (i) comforter (II ii 72); (ii) peace of mind (II iv 63)
QUIT, relieve
QUOTH, says

RAIL'D UPON, abused, scolded
RAMS, battering-rams
RANGE, rank
RANK, both (i) full-grown, luxuriant; and (ii) corrupt
RANKNESS, (i) exuberance; (ii) powerful smell (pun, IV i 59)
RARE, excellent
RATE, 'superfluous rate', excessive price; 'proud rate', excessive value
RAVISH'D, 'Almost with ravish'd list'ning', almost ravished with listening
READ, (i) consider (I i 104); (ii) learn (V v 37)
REAP'D IT, brought it on
RECEIPT OF LEARNING, reception of learned men
RECEIVE AS CERTAIN, accept as truth
RECTIFY, set right
REEK, break into a sweat
RELIGIOUS, strict (IV ii 74)
REMARK'D, noted, talked-about
REND OUR SUBJECTS FROM, force our subjects into disrespect for
RENDER, give
REPAIR, restore
REPEAT, state
REPORT, accusations
REQUIRE, request
REQUITE, repay
RESPITE, delay
REST, remain (V i 55)
REVELS, festivity
REVOKEMENT, cancellation (of the taxes)
RICHARD, King Richard III
RIDDEN, broken in

RIGHT (adv.), very
RIGHTS, 'let 'em have their rights', to give them their due
RIPE, mature
RISING, both (i) rising as a structure, as building continues; and (ii) rising in fame and influence
ROADS, stages (of a journey)
ROSE, a manor belonging to Buckingham
ROUND, 'Clap round fines', impose heavy fines
ROYAL MINDS, devotion to the king
RUB, obstacle, impediment
RUDE STREAM, turbulent current
RULE, control
RUN, 'Is run in', has incurred
RUNNING BANQUET, hasty refreshment; figuratively, a sexual feast (I iv 12); a whipping through the streets (V iv 61)

SABA, the Queen of Sheba (who admired Solomon's wisdom and prosperity; see I Kings x)
SACRING BELL, consecrating bell (here, probably designating the bell rung to summon worshippers to morning prayers)
SAD, serious (Prologue 3, 25, II ii 13, 55, 60)
SALUTE MY BLOOD, exhilarates me
SAMSON . . . SIR GUY . . . COLBRAND, three heroes of legendary strength (Sir Guy was celebrated in romances for slaying the Danish giant Colbrand)
SATISFIED, given satisfaction (for an injury) (II iv 148)
SAW, saw each other (I i 2)
SCARLET, the colour of the Cardinal's robes; 'scarlet sin', heinous sin (from Isaiah i, 18)
SCEPTRE, staff emblematic of monarchy
SCHEDULE, scroll of paper
SCRIBES, public clerks or secretaries
SCRUPLE, doubt
SEAL (n.), 'great seal', emblem of the Lord Chancellor's office; (v.), 'seal it', ratify my loyalty
SECTARY, member of an heretical sect
SEEK ME OUT, concerns me
SEEMING, 'in full seeming', to all appearances
SELF-DRAWING, spun from the self
SELF-METTLE, his own eagerness
SEMBLANCE OF HIS DUTY, a pretence of dutiful kneeling
SENNET, fanfare
SERVICE, 'do my service', send my respects
SET, (i) 'set on', lead on (II iv 241); (ii) seated (III i 74)

SETTLED, 'he's settled, Not to come off, in his displeasure', Wolsey is fixed, not to escape, in the King's displeasure

SEVERAL, (i) different (III i 1 SD); (ii) various (III ii 125)

SHADOW, semblance, insubstantial image

SHORT, brief (IV i 30, V iii 52)

SHOW, spectacle

SHREWD, (i) artful (I iii 7); (ii) malicious (V iii 177)

SHROUDS, sail-ropes of a ship

SICK, (i) envious and unsound (I ii 82); (ii) unhappy (V v 74); 'so sick though for his place', so diseased with pride even if I could have his high position

SICKEN'D, impoverished

SIGN, mark

SIMONY, the buying and selling of church offices

SINGLE, (i) unmarried; (ii) modest, relatively insignificant (pun, I i 15); 'a single part in aught Pertains to the state', an individual's share of the affairs of state; 'a single voice', my individual vote; 'with a single heart', sincerely

SINK, destroy

SIRRAH, term of address used to inferiors

SIT, sit on (IV ii 16)

SLEPT UPON, been blind to

SLIGHTLY, easily

SMALL, low in rank (V i 128)

SMART, pain

SMILE, 'the smile of heaven', God's good graces

SNUFF IT, trim its wick (Wolsey, being called upon simply to clear away impediments to the marriage, plans to end it altogether)

SOCIETY, assembly

SOIL, moral stain

SOLICITED, informed by petitioners

SOMETHING, to some extent; 'something mistaken', to some extent misjudged

SOMETIMES, formerly

SOOTH, 'to say sooth', to tell the truth

SOUND (adj.), loyal (III ii 274, V iii 81–2); (v.), fathom (III ii 436, V ii 13)

SPAN, moment

SPANIARD, Spaniards (Katharine was the daughter of King Ferdinand of Spain)

SPANN'D, measured out, reaching its end

SPARING, being frugal

SPAVIN OR SPRINGHALT, diseases affecting horses' legs

SPEAK, (i) speak of, describe (II iv 140, IV i 61, IV ii 32, 47); (ii) bear witness for, praise (II iv 166, III i 125, IV ii 63); 'spoke to', asked; 'speak thee out', fully describe you; 'speak to', address yourself to

SPEECH, report, public opinion (I ii 154)

SPEED, 'The devil speed him', may the devil make him prosper (reversing the customary blessing of 'God speed'); 'sped to', set out for

SPEEDING, effective

SPELL IN THAT IS OUT, influence of that sort is over

SPICE, dash

SPINSTERS, spinners

SPLEEN, malice

SPLEENY, hot-headed

SPOIL, destroy

SPOONS, set of apostle-spoons, a traditional christening gift; 'spare your spoons', save the expense of buying apostle-spoons

SPORT, entertainment

STAND, remain (II ii 49, IV ii 157); 'stood to', supported

STANDING-BOWLS, bowls with legs

STARVE, die

STATE, (i) dignity (Prologue 3, IV i 36 SD, IV i 93); (ii) chair of state or canopy over it (I ii 8 SD, I iv i SD, I iv 34 SD, V iii i SD); 'keep state', affect grandeur; 'holds his state', maintains his dignity

STATE-STATUES, statues of statesmen

STAY, (i) keep (I i 5); (ii) wait (I i 129, I iii 63, III ii 232, IV ii 105, V iii 97); (iii) stop (III ii 33)

STICK, 'stick them in our will', treat them according to our mere pleasure; 'stick to say', hesitate to say

STILL, always; 'him in eyes Still him in praise', the one seen was always the one praised

STINT, cease to perform

STIRS, 'more stirs against', is more active against

STOCK, trunk of a tree; i.e. mother (V i 22)

STOMACH, arrogance (IV ii 34)

STORE, 'great store', plenty

STRAIGHT, at once

STRAINS, embraces

STRAND, 'the hope o' the' Strand', i.e. apprentices in fashionable shops on the Strand, a London street

STRANGE, foreign (III i 45)

STRANGER, foreigner (I iv 53, II ii 99, II iii 17, II iv 15)

STRETCH'D HIM, rose to his full height

STRIKE, make

STUBBORN, resistant, unyielding

STUDIED PURPOSES, diligent efforts

STUDY, effort

STUFF, (i) qualities of character (I i 58); (ii) textile (III ii 126) (pun on (i) and (ii), III ii 137)

STUMP, stump of a tooth (with sexual suggestion)

SUBSTANCE, material wealth

SUBURBS, lawless areas outside the city's jurisdiction

SUDDEN, immediate; 'on the sudden', all of a sudden; 'sudden commendations', impromptu compliments

SUDDENLY, (i) on the spur of the moment (III i 70); (ii) immediately (V iv 76)

SUE, (i) ask for (II i 70); (ii) apply for (III ii 341)

SUFFER, permit

SUFFERANCE, torment

SUGGESTION, underhand dealings

SUGGESTS, incites, prompts

SUIT, request; 'suit of pounds', petition for money

SUMMONS, i.e. of the Queen, to appear before the assembly

SUPERFLUOUS RATE, excessive price

SUPERSTITIOUS, excessively devoted

SURE, surely

SURVEYOR, overseer of estates

SWITCHES, twigs

TAINT (n.), corruption

TAINTED, 'sorely tainted', severely disgraced

TAKE, 'take up', obstruct; 'take you out', invite you to dance; 'take peace', make my peace; 'take right', succeed; 'better taken', better received

TALKER, maker of empty promises (regarding the hospitality to be shown to Campeius)

TANTA EST ERGA TE MENTIS INTEGRITAS, REGINA SERENISSIMA, so great is the integrity of our purpose toward you, most serene Queen

TARGETS, shields

TAUGHT, 'You are not to be taught', i.e. you already know

TE DEUM, Latin hymn of praise

TELL, count (II i 91)

TEMPER, disposition

TEMPORAL, merely worldly

TENDANCE, attention

TENDER, (i) offer (II ii 101); (ii) value (II iv 116)

TENEMENTS, rented buildings and lands

THEME, reason for rejoicing

THINK TO, expect to

THROE, pang

THROUGHLY, thoroughly

THUNDER, roar, riot

TIED, 'Tied it by letters-patents', confirmed it by a public authorization; 'Tied all the kingdom', brought the entire kingdom into bondage

TIME, continuing course of events (V i 37); 'Good time', good fortune

TIP-STAVES, officers carrying metal-tipped staffs who took convicted men into custody

TO'T, as well (I iii 14)

TONGUE, 'Which action's self was tongue to', which was displayed in the actual events; 'one general tongue', one spokesman for all

TOOL, penis

TOP-PROUD, proud in the highest degree

TOUCH (n.), (i) taint, stain (II iv 155); (ii) hint, inkling (V i 13)

TOUCH ME, affect me

TOWER, Tower of London, where traitors were traditionally imprisoned

TRACE THE CONJUNCTION, follow the marriage

TRACT, course

TRACTABLE OBEDIENCE IS A SLAVE TO EACH INCENSED WILL, docility has given way to anger

TRADUC'D, slandered

TRAIN, (i) retinue (I i 119 SD, II i 136 SD, IV i 37) (ii) trailing portion of a gown (II iii 97, IV i 36 SD, IV i 51, V v 1 SD)

TRAVAIL, labour in childbirth

TREMBLING, i.e. fearfully large

TRIBULATION OF TOWER-HILL, i.e. troublemakers of a rough London district

TRIM, fine (ironical)

TRIPPING, stepping lightly

TROOPS, followers, retainers

TROTH, faith; 'good troth', 'troth and troth', indeed, certainly (with possible pun on 'trot', a contemptuous term for an old woman, II iii 33-4)

TROW, believe

TRUANT, idler

TRUNCHEONERS, youths carrying clubs

TRUST, 'gentleman in trust', trusted servant

TURN THEIR HEARTS, change their feelings

TYPES, marks

UNCONTEMN'D, undespised

UNDER, 'under the King's feet', at the feet of

the King, who is seated on a raised throne; 'Under your hands and seals', with your signed and sealed approval

UNDERSTAND, (i) comprehend things generally; (ii) stand, use their legs (pun, I iii 32)

UNDERSTANDING, (i) considerate and discerning; (ii) standing under the stage, among the 'groundlings' (pun, Prologue 22)

UNDERTAKES, takes charge of

UNFOLDED, revealed

UNHAPPILY, unfavourably

UNPARTIAL, impartial

UPPER GERMANY, inland Germany (referring to any of several uprisings in the 1520s and 1530s)

URGE, press their charges (V iii 48)

USE (n.), 'make use now', take advantage of this opportunity; (v.), 'us'd myself', behaved; 'use so rude behaviour', behave so rudely; 'us'd with honour', treated honourably

VACANT, 'of those virtues vacant', devoid of those virtues

VAIN-GLORY, boastful pride

VALE OF ANDREN, valley of Andren, in France

VALUE (n.), 'in value with', esteemed by

VALUES (v.), 'not values', 'values not', is not worth

VANITY, (i) folly, useless extravagance (I i 54, 85); (ii) trifle (II iii 69); 'trim vanities', handsome nonentities

VEHEMENCY, passion, force

VENT, utter

VERGERS, officials who carry emblems of high office in formal processions

VERILY, truly

VIOLENCE, 'ask with such a violence', demand so vehemently

VIRTUE, 'by that virtue', by virtue of that

VISAGE, 'fair visage', pretty face

VISITATION, visit

VIVA VOCE, with the living voice; i.e. face-to-face, in person

VIZARDS, masks

VOICE, (i) vote (I ii 70, II ii 85, 91, V iii 88); (ii) talk (III ii 405, IV ii 11); 'common voice', general judgment

VOID, empty

VOUCH, allegation

VOUCHSAFE, (i) deign to accept, support (II iii 43); (ii) be so kind as (II iii 71)

WAKING, lively

WANT, lack

WANTON, (i) unrestrainedly triumphant (III ii 241); (ii) frolicsome (III ii 359)

WARRANT, justification

WATER, 'write in water', i.e. soon forget

WAY, (i) profession (I iii 61); (ii) opportunity (III ii 16); (iii) religious persuasion (i.e. anti-Lutheran) (V i 28); 'in your way', (i) in your path; (ii) in your virginal condition (pun, III iii 41); 'Go thy ways', go along; 'that way I am wife in', in my role as a wife

WEAR, spend (II iv 228)

WEEN YOU OF, do you expect

WEIGH, (i) equal in weight or value (I i 11, III ii 259); (ii) 'weigh out', outweigh, compensate for (III i 88); (iii) value (V i 124)

WEIGHT, importance (III i 71)

WELL MET, welcome

WELL SAID, well done

WENCH, affectionate term of address used to female inferiors

WHISPER, confer secretly with

WILL'D ME, asked me to

WILLING, willingly (IV ii 130)

WILLING'ST, most deliberate

WIN, profit (III ii 442, 444)

WINNOWED, dropped in the wind in order to separate the chaff from the grain (i.e. the slander from the truth)

WIT, intelligence, wisdom

WITHAL, (i) with (III ii 130); (ii) in addition (III ii 164)

WITHOUT, outside (V iii 5)

WITNESS, evidence (V i 136)

WONTED, accustomed

WORDS, i.e. empty words (V iii 72)

WORK (n.), (i) affair (V i 18); (ii) fort (V iv 53); (v.), turn (II ii 44)

WORKING (adj.), moving

WORN OUT CHRISTENDOM, used up all Christian fashions

WORSHIP, noble rank

WORTHILY, rightly

WOT, know

WRENCHING, rinsing

WRINGING, torture, suffering

WRIT, wrote, written

WRONG, 'I am not of your wrong', I am not free of the injury your accusations do me

WROUGHT, (i) 'wrought to be', sought to become (III ii 311); (ii) decorated (IV i 36 SD)

YOUNG, recent (III ii 47)